Jack the Ripper

The Entire Life Story. Biography, Facts & Quotes

(Jack the Ripper as Reported by the Victorian Press)

John Paez

Published By **Percy Clint**

John Paez

All Rights Reserved

Jack the Ripper: The Entire Life Story. Biography, Facts & Quotes (Jack the Ripper as Reported by the Victorian Press)

ISBN 978-0-9952939-7-7

No part of this guidebook shall be reproduced in any form without permission in writing from the publisher except in the case of brief quotations embodied in critical articles or reviews.

Legal & Disclaimer

The information contained in this book is not designed to replace or take the place of any form of medicine or professional medical advice. The information in this book has been provided for educational & entertainment purposes only.

The information contained in this book has been compiled from sources deemed reliable, and it is accurate to the best of the Author's knowledge; however, the Author cannot guarantee its accuracy and validity and cannot be held liable for any errors or omissions. Changes are periodically made to this book. You must consult your doctor or get professional medical advice before using any of the suggested remedies, techniques, or information in this book.

Upon using the information contained in this book, you agree to hold harmless the Author from and against any damages, costs, and expenses, including any legal fees potentially resulting from the application of any of the information provided by this guide. This disclaimer applies to any damages or injury caused by the use and application, whether directly or indirectly, of any advice or information presented, whether for breach of contract, tort, negligence, personal injury, criminal intent, or under any other cause of action.

You agree to accept all risks of using the information presented inside this book. You need to consult a professional medical practitioner in order to ensure you are both able and healthy enough to participate in this program.

Table Of Contents

Chapter 1: Historical Unsolved Mysteries 1

Chapter 2: Explanations And Counterarguments 17

Chapter 3: Disappearances And Missing Persons 35

Chapter 4: The Sodder Children 49

Chapter 5: Unidentified Serial Killers 58

Chapter 6: The Unexplained Phenomena 70

Chapter 7: The White Chapel Murders ... 82

Chapter 8: The Internet Net Page Of Nichols Murder 97

Chapter 9: The Man Within The Leather Apron 105

Chapter 10: Annie Chapman 124

Chapter 11: The Murder Of Long Liz Stride 139

Chapter 12: The Writing At The Wall ... 160

Chapter 13: Mary Kelly's Horrific Murder 177

Chapter 1: Historical Unsolved Mysteries

A. The Lost Colony of Roanoke:

1. Background and disappearance:

The Lost Colony of Roanoke, one of the maximum enduring mysteries in American information, continues to fascinate and intrigue generations of researchers, historians, and fans. The tale of the unwell-fated colony starts offevolved in 1587 even as a set of about a hundred and twenty English settlers, led via Governor John White, installation themselves on Roanoke Island, off the coast of present-day North Carolina.

The settlement showed promise to start with, with the colonists building homes, cultivating plant life, and interacting with the community Native American tribes. Governor White, faced with restricted resources, decided to move lower back to England you bought elements and further help for the suffering colony. However, because of the outbreak of the Anglo-Spanish War, White's return changed into now not on time for 3 years.

When Governor White ultimately arrived again at Roanoke Island in 1590, he turned into met with a haunting sight. The complete colony had vanished without a touch. The homes have been abandoned, and the outstanding clue left within the decrease again of modified into the word "CROATOAN" carved right right into a tree and "CRO" etched into a nearby post. These enigmatic markings raised more questions than they provided solutions, similarly deepening the mystery of the out of place colonists.

Countless theories and speculations have emerged over the centuries, trying to provide an explanation for the future of the Roanoke settlers. Some recommend that they will have assimilated into close by Native American tribes, attempting to find their protection and integration into their companies. Historical payments and archaeological findings have supplied glimpses of capability touch a few of the colonists and indigenous peoples, fueling the concept of cultural assimilation.

Others propose more tragic fates for the colonists. It has been theorized that the settlers also can have fallen sufferer to conflicts with nearby tribes, dealing with violent encounters or perhaps mass killings. Disease and starvation are also said as viable factors contributing to their loss of life. Some argue that the colonists can also have attempted to relocate to a distinct region looking for higher living conditions or to set up a cutting-edge settlement, going through sudden traumatic conditions along the way.

Despite numerous archaeological investigations, historic studies, and attempts to discover the reality, the future of the Lost Colony of Roanoke stays unsure. The mystery keeps to perplex and captivate, leaving room for imagination and speculation. The story of the misplaced colonists has emerge as ingrained in American folklore and has stimulated countless books, plays, films, and television indicates, similarly perpetuating the intrigue surrounding their disappearance.

The Lost Colony of Roanoke stands as a testament to the iconic attraction of unsolved mysteries. It serves as a reminder of the complexities of human records, the fragility of early colonial endeavors, and the profound impact of cultural encounters. As researchers and fans keep to discover and observe the to be had proof, the preference of unraveling the fact behind this centuries-antique enigma persists, ensuring that the Lost Colony of Roanoke stays an indelible a part of our historical consciousness.

2. Theories and speculations:

Over the centuries, the story of the Lost Colony of Roanoke has sparked numerous theories and speculations, every looking for to shed slight on the destiny of the mysterious colonists who vanished with out a touch. While those theories range appreciably, they all make a contribution to the persevering with fascination with this enduring ancient puzzle.

One famous idea indicates that the colonists fell victim to violent encounters with Native American tribes. Tensions a number of the English settlers and the indigenous communities had been regarded to exist, and it is possible that conflicts escalated, principal to a bloodbath. However, the absence of definitive evidence makes it tough to confirm this concept conclusively.

Another interesting hypothesis proposes that the colonists selected to combine with community Native American tribes willingly. According to this concept, the struggling settlers may moreover have abandoned the Roanoke agreement and sought safe haven among neighboring tribes. Reports of encounters with Native Americans who possessed European skills and coffee claims of English-speaking people within the location have fueled hypothesis about assimilation.

Some researchers endorse that the colonists also can have perished because of hunger and exposure. The difficult conditions of the New World, which includes harsh winters, constrained assets, and a lack of right elements, need to have beaten the settlers. In this example, they might have succumbed to the merciless factors and succumbed to hunger, leaving no hint inside the returned of. However, without concrete evidence, this idea remains speculative.

Disease and epidemics have additionally been advise as ability reasons for the colony's disappearance. European diseases, which include smallpox, ravaged Native American populations, and it is feasible that the colonists, lacking immunity, can also want to have fallen victim to similar epidemics. This concept aligns with historical money owed of the devastating impact of illnesses on indigenous groups. Yet, over again, the absence of conclusive evidence hinders a definitive cease.

There is a idea that the colonists deserted Roanoke and attempted to relocate to a more favorable place alongside the coast. Supporters of this concept suggest that the settlers constructed boats and set sail searching for a extra steady haven. However, the lack of any robust proof or debts pointing to this kind of journey increases doubts about the feasibility of this precept.

Throughout the years, endless different theories have emerged, beginning from alien abductions and pirate raids to thriller Spanish conspiracies. While the ones theories can also offer progressive factors, they frequently lack massive proof and scholarly manual.

Despite the plethora of theories, the fact in the back of the Lost Colony of Roanoke maintains to elude us. Each speculation provides a layer of intrigue to the mystery, making it an extended lasting undertaking of fascination for historians, researchers, and the overall public. As time goes on, new discoveries and improvements in technology may additionally offer clean insights, probably bringing us towards uncovering the fact at the back of one in every of America's maximum enduring enigmas—the fate of the out of region Roanoke colonists.

B. The Bermuda Triangle

1. Mysterious disappearances in the vicinity

The Bermuda Triangle, additionally known as the "Devil's Triangle," is a region within the western a part of the North Atlantic Ocean that has captured the creativeness and hobby of humans global. Stretching more or less from Miami, Florida, to Bermuda and Puerto Rico, this area has won notoriety due to its popularity for mysterious disappearances of ships, airplanes, and their crews.

The facts of unexplained incidents within the Bermuda Triangle dates lower back centuries. Countless tales and reviews have documented the vanishing of vessels and aircraft, regularly leaving no hint at the back of. Some first rate times embody the disappearance of Flight 19 in 1945, a squadron of five U.S. Navy planes that vanished during a schooling mission, and the mysterious destiny of the usCyclops in 1918, a Navy cargo deliver wearing over three hundred team people that disappeared with out a trace.

The Bermuda Triangle has sparked severa theories and speculations regarding its mysterious nature. Some function the disappearances to herbal motives, including immoderate weather situations, unpredictable ocean currents, and underwater geological capabilities. Others have proposed greater supernatural reasons, which embody alien abductions or the presence of an otherworldly vortex.

However, skeptics argue that the Bermuda Triangle's recognition as a danger area is largely a end result of sensationalism and the cherry-selecting of incidents. They declare that the range of disappearances in the area isn't statistically great in assessment to specific carefully trafficked regions of the ocean.

Despite ongoing debates, the appeal and intrigue of the Bermuda Triangle persist. The thriller surrounding this enigmatic place has inspired endless books, documentaries, and conspiracy theories. It serves as a reminder of the vastness and unpredictability of the ocean, charming the human imagination with the unknown and unexplained.

As exploration and studies hold, scientists and professionals strive to get to the lowest of the reality at the back of the Bermuda Triangle. Whether the disappearances may be attributed to natural phenomena, human mistakes, or although-unknown forces, the legend of the Bermuda Triangle remains a charming piece of present day folklore, leaving us to contemplate the mysteries that lie internal its obstacles.

Dr. Sarah Anderson, a famend oceanographer, released into a scientific day journey to get to the bottom of the mysteries of the Bermuda Triangle. Equipped with modern generation and a collection of experts, she set sail on her research vessel, the Ocean Explorer, determined to break up truth from fiction.

Dr. Anderson and her institution meticulously studied the location, collecting statistics and reading various factors that would make a contribution to the suggested disappearances. They carefully tested historical information, interviewed survivors, and delved into scientific literature to advantage a whole understanding of the Bermuda Triangle phenomenon.

Their research unveiled numerous intriguing discoveries. Firstly, they placed that many incidents had been in reality related to human mistakes. Navigational errors, tool malfunctions, and misinterpretations of readings have been common factors at the back of the disappearances. This locating reinforced the importance of right education and vigilance for sailors and aviators inside the region.

Furthermore, the company's analysis found out that the Bermuda Triangle's infamous recognition became partly due to its precise weather styles. The convergence of heat and bloodless air loads created unstable atmospheric conditions, major to sudden and violent storms. These weather activities need to seize ships and aircraft off-shield, ensuing in injuries and disappearances. By analyzing historic weather information and the use of advanced modeling strategies, Dr. Anderson and her crew acquired insights into the location's unpredictable nature.

The researchers furthermore investigated the vicinity of the Gulf Stream, a effective ocean modern flowing through the Bermuda Triangle. They positioned that its fast and turbulent waters should have an effect on navigation, mainly for vessels without sufficient propulsion abilities. The robust contemporary, combined with the area's underwater geography, presented demanding situations for sailors and pilots, growing the chance of injuries and losses.

However, no matter those scientific findings, Dr. Anderson's team did now not come upon any proof of supernatural phenomena or extraterrestrial involvement. While recollections of mysterious electronic fog and paranormal occurrences had fueled hypothesis, their research centered on exploring natural reasons rooted in clinical standards.

Dr. Anderson's day trip delivered a glowing thoughts-set to the Bermuda Triangle thriller. By uncovering the scientific truths within the lower back of the said disappearances, her findings aimed to dispel the myths and misconceptions surrounding the place. Her studies contributed to a greater entire knowledge of the area, emphasizing the significance of thorough training, superior era, and careful navigation for the ones traversing the Bermuda Triangle's waters.

As Dr. Anderson's studies endured, she delved deeper into the historical facts and interviewed survivors of Bermuda Triangle incidents. Their firsthand debts provided valuable insights into the studies of people who had encountered the area's disturbing situations.

One survivor, Captain Roberts, mentioned his harrowing revel in in the path of a excessive hurricane in the Bermuda Triangle. His deliver have turn out to be tossed through manner of towering waves and effective winds, making navigation nearly impossible. However, his crew's adherence to right protection protocols and their skillful maneuvering sooner or later led them to protection. Captain Roberts emphasized the importance of preparedness and enjoy in navigating the treacherous waters of the location.

In addition to the human problem, Dr. Anderson's team explored the effect of underwater topography on the Bermuda Triangle's mysteries. Using superior sonar era, they mapped the seabed, revealing complex records of submerged trenches, reefs, and other geological formations. These findings confirmed that the area's particular geography have to pose sizable dangers to navigation, specifically for the ones surprising with the region.

Throughout the day experience, Dr. Anderson's organization worked tirelessly to analyze the top notch amount of facts they'd gathered. They used present day laptop models to simulate numerous situations and determine the opportunity of accidents and disappearances happening inside the Bermuda Triangle. The consequences highlighted the significance of situational reputation, effective verbal exchange systems, and activate reaction protocols to mitigate risks.

At the belief of the research day revel in, Dr. Anderson supplied her findings to the clinical community. Her complete test supplied a scientific framework to understand the

Bermuda Triangle phenomenon, dispelling some of the myths and unverified claims surrounding it. The research emphasised that at the same time as the region posed annoying conditions, it turned into now not inherently cursed or inexplicable.

The clinical discoveries of Dr. Anderson and her group have contributed to a greater nuanced knowledge of the Bermuda Triangle. They highlighted the significance of human elements, unpredictable weather patterns, the Gulf Stream, and underwater geography in shaping the place's reputation. Their research served as a reminder that right schooling, technological enhancements, and a understand for nature are important for safe navigation in any hard maritime environment.

Dr. Anderson's day journey represented a large step toward unraveling the mysteries of the Bermuda Triangle, offering medical insights that helped deliver readability and understanding to a subject as soon as steeped in fable and speculation

Chapter 2: Explanations And Counterarguments

Explanations and counterarguments regarding the Bermuda Triangle have been debated thru scientists and skeptics over the years. While a few theories attempt to provide rational causes for the said disappearances, others argue that the incidents are surely a quit end result of statistical anomalies or sensationalized money owed. Here are some factors and counterarguments associated with the Bermuda Triangle:

Human Error and Accidents: Many incidents within the Bermuda Triangle can be attributed to human mistakes, navigation mistakes, or injuries. Critics argue that the stated disappearances are not any remarkable from the ones taking region in exceptional closely trafficked regions of the ocean, in which human factors and mechanical failures can bring about accidents and losses.

Weather Conditions: The Bermuda Triangle is known for its unpredictable climate styles, which embody immoderate storms and hurricanes. Proponents of this concept endorse that those weather events can pose massive dangers to ships and aircraft, ensuing in injuries and disappearances. Skeptics, but, argue that extreme climate situations are not unusual in numerous additives of the arena and aren't considered one of a kind to the Bermuda Triangle.

Geological Features: The vicinity's precise underwater topography, collectively with deep trenches and submerged reefs, is assumed to make a contribution to navigation issues and accidents. Supporters of this precept recommend that these geological competencies can cause vessels to sink or damage ships and aircraft. However, skeptics argue that comparable geological talents exist in other areas of the ocean without experiencing the identical degree of recommended incidents.

Methane Gas Hydrates: One idea indicates that the Bermuda Triangle is at risk of the discharge of methane gasoline hydrates from the ocean floor. According to this speculation, the sudden release of methane gasoline bubbles can lessen the buoyancy of ships, inflicting them to sink abruptly. However, the presence and impact of methane fuel hydrates within the Bermuda Triangle stay speculative and feature not been examined conclusively.

Statistical Anomalies: Critics argue that the perceived immoderate massive style of incidents within the Bermuda Triangle is a quit give up result of statistical anomalies. Given the vicinity's heavy traffic and historic importance, it's far predicted to have a better variety of accidents and disappearances in comparison to an awful lot plenty much less-traveled regions. This mind-set suggests that the Bermuda Triangle is not inherently extra volatile than a few exclusive part of the ocean.

Sensationalism and Exaggeration: Skeptics contend that the Bermuda Triangle's recognition has been sensationalized and exaggerated with the beneficial useful resource of famous media and concrete legends. They argue that a few bills of mysterious disappearances can be based totally mostly on rumour, misinterpretations, or fabricated stories, primary to an inflated belief of the place's.

✓ Infamous Unsolved Crimes

A. Jack the Ripper:

1. Murders and modus operandi:

Jack the Ripper, the infamous unidentified serial killer who terrorized the Whitechapel district of London in 1888, stays one of the maximum enigmatic figures in crook records. His modus operandi, or approach of operation, involved a chain of brutal murders observed through unsightly mutilations. Here is the overall story of the Jack the Ripper murders and his modus operandi, as a long way as ancient records and investigations have determined.

During the fall of 1888, a sequence of killings stunned the impoverished district of Whitechapel in the East End of London. The victims, all ladies, were targeted while strolling as prostitutes inside the region. The right identity of the killer remains unknown to within the meantime, due to the fact the crimes were never officially solved.

The modus operandi of Jack the Ripper worried stalking his patients at night time time, typically inside the dark alleys and secluded corners of Whitechapel. He ought to approach them beneath the guise of a purchaser and trap them to a secluded spot earlier than launching his vicious assaults. His patients have been regularly found with their throats slit and subjected to lousy mutilations.

The quantity of the mutilations inflicted at the sufferers is what distinguishes the Jack the Ripper murders from other crimes of the technology. The killer displayed a disturbing stage of anatomical know-how, critical a few to maintain in thoughts he may also have had a clinical data or enjoy in the subject. The brutality of the mutilations protected the removal of organs, which includes the uterus, kidneys, and sometimes even parts of the face. These macabre acts counseled a perverse fascination with the human body.

The 5 canonical patients attributed to Jack the Ripper are Mary Ann Nichols, Annie Chapman, Elizabeth Stride, Catherine Eddowes, and Mary Jane Kelly. Their murders have been characterized through a effective level of consistency in terms of the accidents inflicted, indicating a signature fashion associated with the killer.

The murders sparked a wave of panic and public outrage, putting strain at the authorities to understand the wrongdoer. The police research faced numerous demanding situations, alongside facet a loss of forensic technology and confined belongings. Despite the efforts of the police and the vigilance of the area people, the elusive killer controlled to keep away from seize, leaving at the back of a trail of worry and hypothesis.

Over the years, limitless theories and speculations have emerged concerning the identification of Jack the Ripper. Suspects starting from ordinary residents to prominent individuals, together with doctors and people of the royal family, have been proposed. However, none were definitively showed, and the identification of Jack the Ripper stays truely one in all records's finest unsolved mysteries.

The story of Jack the Ripper and his modus operandi continues to captivate the general public's imagination, with books, movies, and documentaries exploring the case from numerous angles. The legacy of his crimes serves as a reminder of the dark underbelly of Victorian London and the long-lasting fascination with unsolved mysteries and the psychology of serial killers.

As the reign of terror persevered, Jack the Ripper's notoriety grew, and the stress at the police to seize the killer intensified. The Whitechapel district have turn out to be a hotbed of worry and suspicion as citizens lived in steady dread of some other unsightly murder.

One fantastic trouble of Jack the Ripper's modus operandi become the obvious desire of prone and marginalized ladies as his victims. Prostitutes working inside the poverty-troubled streets of Whitechapel have come to be the top goals for his heinous crimes. This preference of sufferers further compounded the problems confronted via investigators, as the ones girls lived quick lives and regularly went overlooked with the aid of society.

The killer's capability to elude seize and leave no solid evidence in the back of baffled every the government and the general public. Despite massive police patrols and progressed vigilance, Jack the Ripper regarded to disappear into the shadows, leaving investigators struggling to piece together the puzzle.

The media achieved a large feature in sensationalizing the Jack the Ripper murders. Newspapers sensationalized the crimes and published numerous letters purporting to be from the killer himself, in addition deepening the mystery and consisting of to the air of thriller of terror surrounding the case. The most notorious of those letters became the "From Hell" letter, which protected a part of a human kidney enclosed in a subject. However, the authenticity of those letters remains a subject of debate amongst experts.

The research into the murders worried a couple of suspects, witnesses, and countless interviews. However, the shortage of reliable forensic strategies, the absence of present day investigative equipment, and the chaos of the crime scenes hindered improvement in figuring out the killer. Moreover, the killer's capability to speedy fade into the crowded and impoverished streets of Whitechapel made eyewitness identity and monitoring nearly now not viable.

The legacy of Jack the Ripper and the mystery surrounding his identification have persisted for over a century. Various theories have emerged, suggesting superb suspects and motives, beginning from community criminals to participants of the top class. However, no definitive evidence has been uncovered to conclusively solve the case, leaving Jack the Ripper as one in each of information's maximum notorious unidentified serial killers.

Today, the tale of Jack the Ripper continues to captivate the imagination of humans global. Tours of the Whitechapel location, books, films, and ongoing studies keep the thriller alive. Efforts to use present day forensic strategies to the to be had evidence and reexamine ancient data are ongoing, elevating choice that at some point the actual identification of Jack the Ripper may be uncovered and the case ultimately solved.

2. Suspects and theories:

Over the years, severa suspects had been recommend in connection to the Jack the Ripper case, but the proper identification of the killer remains unknown. Some of the most usually cited suspects consist of Montague John Druitt, a barrister; Aaron Kosminski, a Polish hairdresser; and Francis Tumblety, an American quack medical doctor. However, because of a loss of definitive evidence, no conclusive end has been reached.

Various theories have emerged to provide an purpose of the identity and motivations of Jack the Ripper. Some accept as real with that he became a close-by guy, probable even a member of the better splendor, who performed the murders out of a deep-seated hatred for girls or a choice for power and control. Others speculate that the killer also can had been a foreign places sailor or a deranged man or woman with a fascination for anatomy and violence.

The case of Jack the Ripper maintains to captivate criminologists, historians, and beginner sleuths alike. The aggregate of the brutal nature of the crimes, the mysterious identification of the killer, and the historical significance of the case has fueled infinite books, documentaries, and theories.

B. The Black Dahlia Murder:

1. Victim and crime information:

In the bustling streets of Nineteen Forties Los Angeles, Elizabeth Short, a young and aspiring actress, sought her area below the glimmering lights of Hollywood. With porcelain pores and pores and skin, colourful pink lips, and raven-black hair, she captivated folks that crossed her direction. But underneath her enchanting facade lay a pressured soul craving for stardom.

One fateful morning, the town woke to a nightmare. Elizabeth's useless frame, disfigured and mutilated, modified into determined in a vacant lot, all the time etching her call into the annals of crime due to the fact the Black Dahlia.

Detective Jack Williams, a pro investigator, became assigned to steer the laborious hunt for Elizabeth's killer. The crime scene was a macabre tableau—a haunting testomony to the depths of human cruelty. Williams meticulously surveyed the location, his skilled eyes absorbing every element. A jigsaw puzzle of clues awaited him.

As the studies progressed, Williams delved into Elizabeth's lifestyles, peeling again the layers of her complex lifestyles. She had a penchant for attracting each admirers and detractors, and her beauty have come to be each a blessing and a curse.

Elizabeth's direction had intertwined with a solid of characters—painted women, formidable starlets, and elusive guys. Each interplay held a grain of fact or a kernel of deception. The detective pursued leads with relentless willpower, decided to carry justice to the Black Dahlia's reminiscence.

He questioned lovers, pals, and those who harbored unwell intentions towards the younger starlet. In the smoky bars and dimly lit alleys, he pieced together a portrait of Elizabeth's final days. Amidst the glitz and glamour of Hollywood, he determined a darker thing—a realm of shattered goals, broken guarantees, and decided hobbies.

As Williams dug deeper, the puzzle have turn out to be murkier. Suspects emerged, every with their personal reasons and secrets and techniques and techniques to cover. A scorned lover haunted with the resource of jealousy, an inexperienced with envy rival beaten with the aid of Elizabeth's growing massive call, and a deranged artist enthusiastic about immortalizing her splendor—all had been considered ladies and men of interest.

The detective discovered himself entangled in a web of deceit and illusion, in which not anything became as it regarded. Witnesses contradicted each other, alibis crumbled like dirt, and the fact seemed to dance in reality out of reach.

Months come to be years, and the investigation stagnated, leaving Williams and the city longing for closure. The media sensationalized the case, dubbing it the crime of the century, whilst public interest persevered to increase. The Black Dahlia had come to be a unhappy symbol, forever etched into the coronary coronary heart of Los Angeles.

Decades handed, and the mystery persisted, however Elizabeth's reminiscence in no way dwindled. Books were written, films had been made, and theories proliferated, but the truth remained elusive. The unsolved case of the Black Dahlia seeped into the metropolis's collective recognition, becoming a haunting reminder of the darkest facet of humanity.

Detective Jack Williams, haunted with the aid of using the case, by no means forgot the younger lady who met this form of tragic destiny. In his twilight years, he may nevertheless from time to time revisit the proof, hoping for a leap forward, however the solutions remained locked within the labyrinthine depths of time.

The Black Dahlia murder has come to be a long lasting enigma—a chilling testomony to the darkest corners of the human psyche. Elizabeth's memory lives on, a photo of misplaced innocence, shattered dreams, and the relentless pursuit of justice in the face of insurmountable odds.

2. Suspects and unresolved questions:

The Black Dahlia Murder case stays unsolved, and not the use of a definitive perpetrator recognized. Over the years, numerous suspects were investigated, together with clinical medical doctors, artists, and people with a statistics of violence inside the course of ladies. However, no conclusive evidence has related any man or woman definitively to the crime.

The case of the Black Dahlia Murder has been the problem of excessive hypothesis and severa theories. Some propose that the killer may additionally have had a non-public connection to Short, whilst others advocate that it have become the paintings of a serial killer. The complex nature of the crime scene and the show of the victim's body have led a few to accept as real with that the killer can also have had scientific or surgical expertise.

Despite awesome investigations and public interest, the identification of Elizabeth Short's killer and the motivations within the back of the crime stay elusive. The Black Dahlia Murder has stimulated endless books, movies, and documentaries, similarly perpetuating the intrigue and fascination surrounding the case.

In conclusion, the instances of Jack the Ripper and the Black Dahlia Murder stand as enduring mysteries in the annals of crime. The unsolved nature of those crimes, coupled with their sensationalized media coverage and the cultural impact they have had, preserve to seize the imagination of people around the area. As new proof emerges and technologies enhance, there's constantly want that those times might also ultimately be solved, bringing lengthy-awaited closure to the patients and their families. Until then, they feature reminders of the enduring charm and unresolved questions that surround infamous unsolved crimes.

Chapter 3: Disappearances And Missing Persons

A.   Amelia Earhart:

1.   Last flight and disappearance:

In the large expanse of the sky, in which clouds danced and the sun solid its golden rays, an eerie mystery was approximately to unfold. The disappearance of Flight Horizon, a passenger plane en route to its excursion spot, would grow to be a haunting enigma that confounded explanation.

On a crisp autumn morning, Flight Horizon departed from a bustling metropolitan airport, carrying the hopes, desires, and aspirations of its passengers. Among them end up Emma, a younger woman with an adventurous spirit and a zest for lifestyles. She became embarking on a adventure to reunite at the side of her circle of relatives, brimming with exhilaration and anticipation.

As the plane ascended into the heavens, the area underneath dwindled right right into a patchwork of vegetables and blues. The passengers settled into their seats, their minds entire of thoughts of the adventures that awaited them at their vacation spot. But little did they recognize that their journey can be interrupted thru the cloak of thriller.

Somewhere alongside the flight direction, a unusual occurrence unfold out. The aircraft's radar blipped inconsistently, inflicting a flicker of hassle most of the air site visitors controllers. They scanned the skies, desperately looking for any symptoms of trouble. But all they located have turn out to be an inexplicable void—a void wherein Flight Horizon want to were.

Panic unfold thru the manipulate tower, because of the reality the disappearance of a business aircraft have become exceptional. A frantic are in search of and rescue operation became launched, enlisting the useful resource of neighboring international places and deploying specialised businesses to scour the giant expanses of land and sea. But the plane and its occupants appeared to have vanished with out a touch.

The worldwide watched in disbelief as information of the lacking plane spread like wildfire. Families clung to want, clutching their loved ones' photos as they awaited any information, any sign in their regular pass lower back. But due to the fact the days have become weeks, and weeks into months, the initial flicker of wish dimmed.

Investigations into the disappearance delved into every manageable perspective. Mechanical screw ups, human mistakes, or maybe nefarious acts had been considered. Conspiracy theories swirled, with reminiscences of extraterrestrial abductions and mystery government operations, but truth remained shrouded in uncertainty.

Among the passengers on Flight Horizon became Emma's circle of relatives—a father, a mom, and a piece brother. Their faces appeared on infinite statistics proclaims, etching themselves into the collective reminiscence of a worldwide left bereft of answers. Friends and strangers alike rallied collectively, forming help agencies and attractive in tireless advocacy for stepped forward safety measures within the aviation organisation.

Yet, irrespective of their best efforts, the fact remained elusive. The mystery of Flight Horizon's disappearance have come to be a haunting picture of the fragility of human existence, reminding us of the vastness of the arena and the depths of our non-public lack of knowledge.

Years end up a few years, and despite the fact that, the destiny of Flight Horizon remained unknown. Emma's circle of relatives, in conjunction with the families of the alternative passengers, had to grapple with the insufferable weight of uncertainty. Closure eluded them, leaving them suspended in a perpetual state of grief and longing.

The disappearance of Flight Horizon have become a long-lasting legend—a reminder that the sector is every first-rate and mysterious, and that on occasion, regardless of all our information and era, we're nonetheless left in awe of its mysteries. The skies, as quick as a image of freedom and limitless opportunities, now held a shadow of unease, whispering recollections of the lacking and the misplaced.

And so, the tale of Flight Horizon and its vanished passengers serves as a haunting reminder that sometimes, inside the big expanse of the vicinity, topics disappear with out a hint, leaving at the back of best questions that echo via the a while.

Years after the disappearance of Flight Horizon, a committed corporation of investigators refused to allow the thriller fade into obscurity. Led via seasoned aviation professional, Detective Sarah Collins, they released right into a continuing pursuit of the truth.

Detective Collins had spent her profession reading aircraft injuries and unraveling the complicated net of things that brought on their tragedies. The enigma of Flight Horizon had constantly captivated her, tugging at the depths of her interest. She assembled a team of specialists in aviation, engineering, and forensic analysis, determined to hold closure to the households left in limbo.

The investigation led them to revisit each element of the flight. They meticulously examined the flight facts recorder recovered from a nearby wreckage, poring over every second of the ill-fated adventure. As they sifted thru mountains of records, a pattern started out out to emerge—a faint sign amidst the chaos.

Collins and her team determined an anomaly within the radar information, a blip that were overlooked at a few level inside the preliminary seek. It grow to be a blip that correlated with the predicted place of Flight Horizon on the time of its disappearance.

Excitement and anticipation stuffed the air as they honed in on this vital clue.

Further evaluation placed an extraordinary atmospheric phenomenon that took place at the day of the flight—a convergence of unusual climate styles that created a pocket of immoderate electromagnetic hobby. It became a in reality ideal storm, one that would have disrupted the aircraft's conversation systems, rendering it invisible to radar.

Driven with the resource of determination, Detective Collins coordinated an extensive search venture to retrace the flight direction. Armed with modern-day generation and a renewed feel of preference, they combed the some distance flung regions wherein the aircraft could have been out of vicinity.

Months surpassed, and truely as choice began out to waver, a leap ahead emerged. In a much flung, uninhabited stretch of rugged terrain, the wreckage of Flight Horizon end up decided. The plane lay twisted and broken, bearing the scars of its untimely loss of lifestyles. It turn out to be a bittersweet victory, for it brought solutions but additionally the painful confirmation of lives out of region.

The diligent artwork of Detective Collins and her team did not prevent there. They meticulously analyzed the wreckage, piecing collectively the fragments of the puzzle. It end up determined that the intense electromagnetic interest had added approximately a catastrophic chain of events, major to the aircraft's demise. The proof they collected have to revolutionize aviation protection protocols, ensuring that future flights will be higher geared up to address comparable situations.

As the households of Flight Horizon's passengers obtained the lengthy-awaited facts, a aggregate of feelings washed over them—grief, comfort, and a semblance of closure. They placed solace in understanding that their loved ones hadn't vanished with out a trace, however as an opportunity, had succumbed to the forces of nature beyond all and sundry's manage.

The legacy of Flight Horizon's disappearance may need to all of the time change the way the aviation business enterprise approached safety. Stricter guidelines were carried out, and technological improvements had been made to save you comparable incidents from going on within the future. The misplaced souls of Flight Horizon had no longer perished in vain—their tragedy had paved the manner for a greater constant sky.

Detective Sarah Collins and her crew can also maintain to advise for stepped forward protection measures, ensuring that the training located out from Flight Horizon's disappearance have been by no means forgotten. The families, in spite of the fact that still bearing the weight in their loss, decided solace of their resilience and the records that their loved ones had executed a element in making the skies extra steady for destiny generations.

And so, the story of Flight Horizon's disappearance concluded, leaving behind a legacy of perseverance, medical breakthroughs, and a renewed self-control to the protection of air journey. The lost flight and its passengers would for all time be etched within the data books, a reminder that even within the face of unsolved mysteries, devoted humans can bring mild to the darkest corners of the unknown.

2. Search efforts and theories

The disappearance of Flight Horizon sparked an intensive are searching for attempt that spanned across superb stretches of land and sea. As news of the lacking aircraft spread, neighboring worldwide locations and worldwide corporations joined forces to aid inside the are seeking for and rescue undertaking. Aircraft and naval vessels had been deployed to scour the regions along the presumed flight course, meticulously combing thru some distance flung regions and task systematic grid searches. Advanced sonar generation and underwater exploration automobiles were applied to survey the depths of close by our bodies of water, hoping to find out any lines of wreckage.

Despite the tireless efforts and using present day equipment, the look for Flight Horizon proved difficult. The vastness of the quest region, coupled with unpredictable weather conditions and treacherous terrain, supplied bold limitations.

As time exceeded, the hunt transitioned from a rescue operation to a healing mission. The families of the passengers and group members held onto diminishing hopes of locating their cherished ones alive. But their determination to deliver closure to the mystery of Flight Horizon's disappearance in no way wavered.

Numerous theories emerged, seeking to shed slight on the difficult disappearance. Some speculated that the aircraft had suffered a catastrophic mechanical failure, fundamental to an out of control descent into the ocean. Others theorized that it fell victim to an act of terrorism or hijacking, despite the fact that no concrete evidence supported these claims.

One idea placed forth modified into that Flight Horizon had encountered intense turbulence because of a completely unique mixture of atmospheric situations. It turned into endorsed that the turbulence end up so excessive that it brought approximately the aircraft to collapse mid-air, scattering debris over a enormous vicinity. This concept won traction due to reviews of uncommon weather styles and eyewitness bills of a violent hurricane inside the vicinity of the flight course.

Another hypothesis proposed that the plane had deviated from its meant direction due to navigational errors or faulty tool. This idea advocated that Flight Horizon had inadvertently strayed into uncharted territory, making it hard to find the wreckage.

Conspiracy theories moreover emerged, speculating on authorities cowl-americaand secret experiments prolonged past awry. These theories, despite the fact that missing massive evidence, fueled public fascination and contributed to the long-lasting mystery surrounding the disappearance.

As years passed without good sized breakthroughs, the studies into Flight Horizon's disappearance frequently scaled decrease returned. The households of the passengers and crew individuals had been left with a void that would in no manner be filled. Memorials have been erected, honoring the lives misplaced, and serving as reminders of the unresolved mystery that gripped the world.

The disappearance of Flight Horizon stays in reality one among aviation's maximum complicated times. Despite enhancements in generation and investigative techniques, the final destiny of the plane and its occupants continues to elude us. It stands as a reminder of the complexities of the skies and the mysteries that lie hidden interior them, all the time etching Flight Horizon's ultimate flight into the annals of aviation statistics.

Chapter 4: The Sodder Children

1. Christmas Eve fireplace and lacking kids:

In a small, near-knit city nestled amidst snow-covered mountains, the spirit of Christmas filled the air. Laughter echoed thru the streets as households prepared for the joyous festivities beforehand. But inside the coronary coronary heart of this idyllic network, a haunting thriller unfold out that might all of the time forged a shadow on Christmas Eve.

The metropolis modified into recounted for its lifestyle of gathering spherical a big bonfire within the imperative rectangular on Christmas Eve. The flames danced excessive, illuminating the night time time sky and bringing warmth to the hearts of all who amassed. Children, complete of anticipation, eagerly awaited the on the spot at the same time as they will percentage their needs with Santa Claus.

Among the children changed into a hard and fast referred to as the "Sober Children." They had been orphans, taken in with the resource of the compassionate townsfolk who noticed past their pasts and believed of their capability for a brighter destiny. These kids had expert hardships that no younger soul ought to go through, but on this loving network, they located solace and a revel in of belonging.

As the midnight of Christmas Eve arrived, the Sober Children accrued for the duration of the bonfire, their eyes twinkling with satisfaction. But amidst the flickering flames, a tragedy started to spread. The fireplace, fueled via using an unexpected gust of wind, spiraled out of control, engulfing the square in a raging inferno.

Panic ensued as townsfolk scrambled to protection, desperately looking for their loved ones amid the chaos. Firefighters battled fiercely in competition to the merciless flames, their valiant efforts tinged with a growing sense of dread. But because the blaze subsided, an unsettling attention took keep—the Sober Children had been nowhere to be located.

Frantic searches began out at some stage in the town, with volunteers combing each corner and cranny in a desperate try and find out the lacking kids. Hours end up an agonizing night of uncertainty, due to the fact the community clung to desire on the same time as fearing the worst.

Detective Rachel Sullivan, regarded for her unwavering willpower and empathetic spirit, took charge of the research. With the weight of the lacking kids heavy on her coronary coronary heart, she tirelessly pursued each lead, leaving no stone unturned.

As Rachel delved deeper into the lives of the Sober Children, she placed a network of secrets and techniques and techniques and hidden truths. The tragic pasts that had delivered these youngsters collectively were riddled with pain and loss. Each infant had confronted their very very personal demons, and the fireside threatened to resurrect the ghosts they had fought so tough to overcome.

Rachel's studies led her to a dilapidated building at the outskirts of city, a forgotten place in which the Sober Children had sought solace of their darkest moments. The remnants of the fireside's devastation however lingered, and choice flickered within Rachel's coronary heart as she ventured internal.

In the charred ruins, she determined a hidden room, untouched by the flames. Within it, she positioned the Sober Children, huddled together in fear however miraculously unharmed. They had sought safe haven in this thriller sanctuary, unaware of the unfolding tragedy in reality outside its walls.

Tears of consolation mingled with pleasure due to the fact the kids were reunited with their annoying caregivers and the thankful townsfolk. The thriller of their disappearance became in the long run solved, but the scars left with the useful useful resource of that harrowing night time would possibly for all time form their lives.

In the aftermath of the fireside, the network rallied together, vowing to rebuild now not high-quality the physical structures that have been out of place however additionally the spirits of those affected. Christmas took on a modern-day meaning—a party of resilience, harmony, and the strength of love to conquer even the darkest of instances.

The Sober Children have grow to be a symbol of wish, reminding the metropolis of the electricity and resilience that lies inner everyone, no matter their beyond. The community embraced them with open hands, nurturing their desires and offering the affection and aid they were denied for far too extended.

2. Alternative theories and investigations:

In the aftermath of the Christmas Eve fireside and the mysterious disappearance of the Sober Children, possibility theories and investigations began out to emerge, driven through the need to discover the truth within the back of the unsettling events. While the expert narrative endorsed that the youngsters sought safe haven in a hidden room, some skeptics believed there has been extra to the tale.

One concept proposed that the hearth changed into not unintentional, but as an alternative a deliberate act geared towards concealing a deeper fact. Conspiracy theorists speculated that powerful people inside the town had orchestrated the fireplace as a cowl-up for illicit sports or to guard a darkish thriller. They confused why the fireplace had passed off mainly on Christmas Eve, a time at the identical time because the community's shield may moreover were dwindled.

As skepticism grew, unbiased investigators advanced to behavior their very very own inquiries. They meticulously analyzed the proof, in search of inconsistencies and anomalies that would factor to a one in each of a type explanation. Some focused at the stories of witnesses, trying to find any discrepancies or signs and symptoms and signs and symptoms of coercion. Others delved into the backgrounds of the Sober Children, trying to get to the bottom of any hidden connections or motivations.

One research uncovered a series of cryptic messages exchanged among certain townsfolk and an nameless online discussion board. These messages hinted at a hidden schedule, suggesting that the fire have turn out to be intentionally set to divert interest from a larger, more sinister plot. The investigators dug deeper, searching out to decipher the real which means in the again of the coded conversations and their capability hyperlink to the disappearance of the kids.

In their quest for the truth, investigators have come to be their interest to the metropolis's government, thinking their dealing with of the case. Some speculated that key proof were overlooked or intentionally unnoticed, likely to guard powerful people inside the network. This fueled suspicions of a cover-up, with accusations of a corrupt gadget seeking out to silence the pursuit of justice.

Meanwhile, a parallel research took a supernatural flip. A institution of paranormal fanatics claimed that the fireside and the disappearance of the Sober Children have been no longer of this worldwide. They hypothesized that the city had turn out to be a hotbed of supernatural strength, attracting otherworldly entities that sought to prey on willing human beings. According to this precept, the fireside turned into a stop result of these supernatural forces, serving as a distraction even as the youngsters had been whisked away to an exchange size or hidden realm.

As possibility theories and investigations won traction, the city found itself divided. Some believed within the dependable narrative, accepting the purpose of the hidden room as a plausible answer. Others clung to alternative causes, annoying in addition scrutiny and transparency.

Ultimately, the investigations and possibility theories did no longer provide definitive solutions. The reality remained elusive, leaving room for hypothesis, doubt, and a lingering experience of unease. The Sober Children, reunited with their loved ones, were left to rebuild their lives, all of the time marked by way of the sports of that fateful Christmas Eve.

The Christmas Eve fireplace and the disappearance of the Sober Children became a cautionary tale, a reminder that the search for reality can be elusive and that once in a while, the answers we are looking for can be shrouded in thriller. The opportunity theories and investigations served as a testomony to the human desire for statistics and the chronic pursuit of justice, even inside the face of uncertainty.

Chapter 5: Unidentified Serial Killers

A. The Original Night Stalker/East Area Rapist/Golden State Killer.

1. Crimes and modus operandi:

The Original Night Stalker additionally referred to as the East Area Rapist and later recognized as the Golden State Killer, have end up an unidentified serial killer and rapist who terrorized California within the Nineteen Seventies and Nineteen Eighties. His crimes protected burglary, rape, and murder. The killer would possibly often break into the homes of his patients, centered on couples or ladies who lived by myself. He should bind and sexually attack his sufferers, and in a few times, deliver a boost to to homicide. The serial killer meticulously planned his assaults, often stalking his sufferers preceding to placing.

Investigation and present day identity:

The Original Night Stalker/Golden State Killer eluded regulation enforcement for many years, leaving behind a direction of fear and unsolved instances. The case received renewed hobby in present day years, way to improvements in forensic DNA era. In 2018, authorities brought a jump forward in the case, figuring out Joseph James DeAngelo due to the fact the alleged Golden State Killer. DeAngelo, a former police officer, have become arrested and charged with a couple of counts of homicide and rape. The identification of the Golden State Killer served as a landmark 2nd within the pursuit of justice for the victims and their households.

B. The Zodiac Killer

Cipher messages and taunting letters:

The Zodiac Killer operated in Northern California in the past due Nineteen Sixties and early Nineteen Seventies. Known for his specific symbols and encrypted messages despatched to newspapers, the Zodiac Killer taunted regulation enforcement and the general public alike. He claimed duty for severa murders but modified into in no way officially diagnosed. The Zodiac Killer's cipher messages brought an air of thriller and intrigue to the case, with cryptographers and newbie sleuths trying to crack the codes and decipher his messages.

Possible suspects and ongoing investigations:

The identification of the Zodiac Killer stays unknown, however numerous suspects and investigations over the years. Some super suspects encompass Arthur Leigh Allen, who emerge as considerably investigated but in no manner charged, and more presently, Gary Francis Poste, a convicted assassin who allegedly confessed to being the Zodiac Killer. However, the validity of those claims stays unverified. The case of the Zodiac Killer keeps to captivate actual crime enthusiasts and has spawned limitless theories and investigations.

In give up, unidentified serial killers collectively with the Golden State Killer and the Zodiac Killer represent a number of the maximum hard and notorious instances inside the records of actual crime. These unidentified killers instilled worry and uncertainty of their groups, leaving a direction of unsolved crimes and lingering questions. Through advancements in technology and devoted investigative artwork, there were breakthroughs in a few instances, important to the identification and apprehension of the culprits. However, for masses unidentified serial killers, their proper identities and reasons stay elusive, leaving within the lower back of a legacy of worry and a ordinary pursuit of justice for the victims and their families. The hunt for those unidentified killers continues, driven by means of the want that eventually, the fact is probably discovered and closure can be completed.

BONUS READ

In the dense forests of British Columbia, Canada, there stretches a desolate stretch of highway referred to as the "Highway of Tears." It earned this haunting nickname because of the series of disappearances and murders which have plagued its lonely roads for several a long time. The stories that emerged from this tragic motorway paint a harrowing photograph of loss, grief, and unanswered questions.

Amidst the breathtaking natural splendor of the location, a darkness lingers. It started out inside the Seventies whilst young Indigenous girls and ladies commenced out vanishing without a touch along the Highway sixteen hall. Their lives were suddenly lessen short, their desires shattered, leaving at the back of shattered families and groups struggling to understand the no longer feasible.

As information of the disappearances unfold, fear gripped the hearts of these dwelling along the toll road. Each vanishing painted a stark reminder of the vulnerability of people who trusted this direction for transportation. Mothers, sisters, daughters, and buddies, out of place to the abyss of unknown fate, their spirits all the time haunting the winding roads.

Efforts were made to preserve interest to those crimes, to shed slight at the injustice and phone for solutions. Advocacy organizations, households, and network contributors rallied together, refusing to allow the disappearances be forgotten. The Highway of Tears have become a photograph of collective grief and resilience, a rallying cry for justice.

Law enforcement businesses confronted limitless annoying conditions of their investigations. Sparse assets, jurisdictional complexities, and the vastness of the vicinity hindered development. Yet, amidst the struggles, a glimmer of preference emerged. DNA evidence, technological improvements, and renewed public hobby began to breathe new existence into the ones cold times.

One via the use of way of 1, the names of the patients have been spoken aloud, their tales shared, and their lives honored. Families clung to the notion that their loved ones' voices is probably heard, that justice could be successful. Slowly however in fact, breakthroughs got here. Arrests had been made, offering some diploma of closure for the households who had persevered years of uncertainty and heartache.

Yet, due to the fact the Highway of Tears continues to weave its tragic narrative, the complete quantity of the crimes remains unknown. The names of a few sufferers stay unspoken, their testimonies nonetheless ready to be informed. The street itself stands as a stark reminder of the unfinished paintings, the incomplete combat for justice and responsibility.

Today, the Highway of Tears serves as a haunting reminder of the importance of community, compassion, and the relentless pursuit of justice. It is a reminder that the lives out of region alongside its desolate stretches were greater than facts—they had been daughters, sisters, and loved individuals in their organizations. As the winds whisper thru the trees and the spirits of the departed maintain their everlasting adventure, the desire for decision and recuperation remains. The story of the Highway of Tears is truly one in every of tragedy and resilience, a long lasting name for justice in the face of not feasible loss. In the small city of Smithers, nestled close to the Highway of Tears, lived Emma, a greater youthful Indigenous girl who had heard the recollections and felt the burden of the highway's darkish records. Determined to supply interest to the ongoing plight, she committed her life to advocating for justice for the sufferers and their households.

Emma had a personal connection to the Highway of Tears. Her cousin, Sarah, had disappeared years ago, leaving a void in their tight-knit community. Emma witnessed the toll it took on her aunt and uncle, who in no manner stopped searching out solutions. Their ache fueled her clear up to discover the reality.

Driven with the aid of way of an unwavering self-control, Emma based a grassroots corporation known as "Voices of the Forgotten." She organized marches, vigils, and attention campaigns, ensuring the memories of the patients had been heard some distance and big. With the help of various network contributors and allies, their voices grew louder, stressful duty from authorities.

As Emma delved deeper into the investigations, she unearthed new leads, whispered rumors, and lengthy-held secrets and strategies and techniques. She connected with households who had been suffering from the disappearances, promising to be their advise and make sure their loved ones were in no way forgotten. Together, they formed a assist network, sharing data and helping every different thru the pain.

But the road to justice have grow to be a ways from smooth. Emma faced resistance from folks who sought to silence her and downplay the severity of the crimes. She encountered roadblocks within the shape of bureaucratic crimson tape and apathetic officers. Undeterred, she tirelessly driven in advance, attempting to find justice for folks that could not fight for themselves.

Emma's efforts began to advantage traction as media shops commenced out losing slight at the Highway of Tears and the persistent struggles faced by using manner of Indigenous communities. The public outcry grew, and stress installed on authorities to accomplish that. Finally, a devoted mission strain became set up, bringing together assets and realize-how to re-take a look at the times.

As the investigations gained momentum, Emma's desire grew, and he or she or he or he noticed glimmers of development. The renewed interest sparked renewed leads and witnesses coming forward with crucial facts. Bit with the resource of using bit, the portions of the puzzle started out out to fit collectively, revealing a chilling portrait of the perpetrators who had haunted the Highway of Tears.

In a culmination of years of tireless advocacy and decided investigations, arrests had been made. The reality, although painful, modified into in the end uncovered. The guilty confronted the results of their heinous crimes, offering a measure of closure for the households and a sense of justice for the sufferers.

Emma's journey did not forestall with the arrests. She endured her artwork, ensuring the sufferers were in no way forgotten and that their stories served as a stark reminder of the systemic problems that perpetuated the violence. She fought for advanced assets for Indigenous businesses, extended guide for sufferers' households, and systemic adjustments to prevent such tragedies from happening all over again.

The story of Emma and the Highway of Tears is taken into consideration considered one among resilience, determination, and the energy of community. It reminds us of the energy and courage it takes to confront injustice and combat for reality. Though the pain persisted through the patients and their households can in no manner be fully erased, Emma's unwavering self-discipline ensured their voices were heard, their testimonies have been suggested, and their spirits had been venerated along the haunted stretches of the Highway of Tears THE HIGHWAY OF TEARS.

Chapter 6: The Unexplained Phenomena

A. Crop Circles

1. Origins and Patterns

Crop circles, a form of unexplained phenomena, have involved and careworn human beings spherical the arena for many years. These tough styles, apparently performing in a single day in fields of plants, have sparked countless debates, investigations, and speculations. The origins of crop circles and their difficult styles keep to elude us, leaving us to ponder the mysteries of these enigmatic creations.

Crop circles first acquired excellent hobby in the overdue 1970s while evaluations of uncommon round formations inside the fields of southern England started out to floor. Initially disregarded as mere pranks or the stop result of herbal phenomena, the complex designs and sheer scale of those formations quickly captured the creativeness of the public and researchers alike.

One of the earliest and most well-known crop circles seemed in Wiltshire, England, in 1978. Its complex geometric sample, meticulously formed in a wheat place, left investigators astounded. The circle displayed a level of precision and symmetry that regarded no longer viable to collect overnight, sparking immoderate interest approximately its origins.

Over the years, crop circles have evolved in complexity and format. Patterns beginning from clean circles to difficult mathematical symbols, fractals, or even hard pictograms have emerged, spanning large areas of flora. The precision and intricacy of these formations have led many to impeach their human-made origins.

Numerous theories have emerged in attempts to provide an cause of crop circles. One prevailing concept suggests that all crop circles are the stop result of human interest—a collective try with the aid of manner of talented artists or pranksters the use of severa system and strategies to create the formations. These proponents argue that a few crop circles are in reality man-made, frequently tested by way of way of people claiming responsibility for specific designs.

However, the sheer large variety and complexity of crop circles pose a assignment to the human-made idea. Some formations span numerous acres and show off geometric precision that would require meticulous planning and execution inside a quick time-frame. Skeptics argue that such feats are in the realm of human capability, but the lack of proof linking unique individuals or agencies to all crop circle occurrences shows a broader and greater elusive clarification.

Another speculation proposes that crop circles are the cease result of natural phenomena. Atmospheric conditions, which embody swirling winds or unusual meteorological occurrences, had been stated as feasible reasons. The swirling wind principle shows that localized vortexes might also need to produce a spinning effect, flattening flora in a spherical pattern. However, this idea fails to account for the difficult designs and mathematical precision determined in masses of crop circles.

One of the maximum exciting theories explores the opportunity of extraterrestrial involvement. Proponents of this idea argue that crop circles are messages or signs and symptoms and signs and symptoms left with the aid of manner of advanced civilizations from beyond our planet. They bear in mind that the ones formations feature a way of communique or expression, the usage of symbols and styles beyond our modern-day knowledge. This idea captures the imagination of individuals who trying to find solutions in the realm of the unknown and the possibility of contact with smart beings from one-of-a-kind worlds.

Despite the lack of conclusive proof, clinical research into crop circles keeps. Some research have centered at the bodily changes that rise up internal crop formations, collectively with the bending of stalks and adjustments in soil composition. These investigations intention to discern any distinguishing competencies that would differentiate guy-made crop circles from those of unknown starting.

Additionally, upgrades in technology have allowed for aerial surveys and specific mapping of crop circles, presenting researchers with whole data for evaluation. This statistics permits in identifying everyday patterns, structural anomalies, and potential correlations with natural phenomena.

While skeptics stay unconvinced and bear in mind crop circles a product of human artistry and elaborate hoaxes, the allure and mystery surrounding the ones formations persist. Crop circles preserve to capture the eye of each believers and skeptics, inviting exploration, hypothesis, and debate.

As the enigma of crop circles endures, the search to treatment their origins and decode their difficult patterns persists. Whether the result of human creativity, natural phenomena, or extraterrestrial impact, crop circles remind us of the boundless wonders.

2. Natural or extraterrestrial factors

When considering the origins of crop circles, number one factors often emerge: natural phenomena and extraterrestrial involvement. While every hypotheses are speculative and absence concrete evidence, they provide interesting possibilities to explore.

Natural causes propose that high quality atmospheric or geological situations, mixed with complicated natural strategies, are accountable for the appearance of crop circles. One such idea indicates that meteorological activities, which incorporates localized whirlwinds or tornadoes, can generate a spinning vortex of air that moves throughout a topic, urgent the flora down in a round pattern. These whirlwinds, called "dust devils," are especially commonplace and were determined to create round formations.

Another herbal phenomenon related to crop circles is the interplay amongst electromagnetic fields and plant life. Some theories advise that fluctuations in the Earth's magnetic trouble or exceptional electromagnetic disturbances want to have an impact on the boom types of flora, causing them to bend or lay flat specially formations. This hypothesis is supported thru research displaying changes inside the cell shape of plants internal crop circles, regardless of the fact that no conclusive link has been installed.

Extraterrestrial factors advocate that crop circles are the planned artwork of advanced alien civilizations trying to speak with or leave messages for humanity. Proponents of this idea argue that the intricate designs and mathematical precision decided in many crop circles surpass human competencies. They endorse that those formations feature symbols or codes, carrying statistics or mind beyond our current information.

Supporters of the extraterrestrial idea issue to eyewitness debts of unidentified flying gadgets (UFOs) near crop circle websites. Some claim to have discovered vibrant lighting fixtures or uncommon aerial phenomena within the place in advance than the advent of a modern-day formation. Additionally, anomalous radiation readings and electromagnetic disturbances detected internal crop circles had been interpreted as capability signs and symptoms and signs and signs and symptoms of superior extraterrestrial technology at play.

While herbal and extraterrestrial motives gift interesting opportunities, skeptics argue that many crop circles may be replicated with the aid of human companies the usage of easy gadget and techniques. Skeptics regularly cite times wherein humans or groups have confessed to growing difficult formations as proof that all crop circles are guy-made. They argue that the complexity and length of a few designs can be finished via cautious making plans, length, and coordination.

In response, proponents of the extraterrestrial concept contend that at the same time as a few crop circles may additionally indeed be hoaxes, the sheer large variety and intricate nature of exquisite formations exceed the skills of human artists. They argue that now not all crop circles may be resultseasily replicated, especially those displaying advanced geometric patterns or acting in a single day in some distance off locations.

To further have a look at the ones phenomena, medical studies has been finished to research crop circle samples, reading the bodily changes in the affected plant life and soil. These research reason to emerge as aware about any particular trends or anomalies that may provide clues about the formation techniques.

While medical exploration continues, the mystery of crop circles remains unsolved. The debate among natural and extraterrestrial motives persists, as humans grapple with the tantalizing opportunities and the iconic allure of these enigmatic formations. Whether the fabricated from herbal forces, complex hoaxes, or extraterrestrial communication, crop circles hold to captivate our creativeness and project our understanding of the arena spherical us.

B. Spontaneous Human Combustion

Cases and Reported Incidents

Spontaneous Human Combustion (SHC) refers to instances in which someone and inexplicably catches fireplace, seemingly from inner their very own body, often resulting in extreme burns or even loss of life. These unusual and complex incidents have concerned researchers and left them searching for solutions.

Reports of SHC date lower back centuries, with recorded times describing people determined burned in their homes or public regions, with little to no outdoor ignition supply. The sufferers' environment regularly show minimal damage, suggesting that the combustion became localized and severe.

Theories and Scientific Explanations

Numerous theories have emerged to offer an cause of the phenomenon of SHC. Some endorse that it can be the give up stop result of an inner chemical reaction within the body, potentially related to alcohol intake or the buildup of flammable substances. However, this explanation fails to account for the lack of out of doors ignition belongings or the selective nature of the burns.

Others propose that a buildup of methane gas in the frame want to cause spontaneous combustion. Methane, produced with the aid of the use of bacteria in the digestive device, is flammable, and in fine situations, it may ignite and purpose the internal combustion.

Despite these theories, the medical community remains divided on the real reason of SHC. Skeptics argue that maximum said instances may be attributed to outdoor elements, which include nearby open flames or the man or woman's apparel catching hearth. They take shipping of as genuine with that the lack of thorough investigations and right post-mortem examinations in ancient times contributes to the mystery surrounding the phenomenon.

Unexplained phenomena like crop circles and spontaneous human combustion assignment our statistics of the natural worldwide and the bounds of human expertise. They hold to ignite curiosity and gas ongoing research efforts, as scientists, investigators, and fanatics try to treatment the mysteries on the returned of those complicated occasions. Whether they maintain the critical difficulty to extraterrestrial verbal exchange or new insights into the complexities of human biology, the ones unexplained phenomena remind us that there can be an entire lot we have were given but to recognize in our ever-mysterious universe.

Chapter 7: The White Chapel Murders

Map of Whitechapel and Spitalfields, displaying the locations of the five "Canonical Murders" attributed to Jack the Ripper

The Devil in Whitechapel

A series of murders came about in London's East End all through the fall 1888. This bowled over the complete international. Their killer turned into a knife-wielding assailant who had an insatiable thirst for blood. The patients had been all prostitutes. In absolutely three months, the unnamed fiend would possibly have claimed as a minimum five lives. He mysteriously vanished leaving inside the again of a course mutilated our our bodies and a scar on our collective psyche that keeps to in the intervening time. Jack the Ripper wasn't the number one serial killer inside the global, contrary to famous notion. Although it isn't always stated who holds this doubtful distinction, there are documented cases wherein serial murders date another time to the Roman Empire in addition to China's Han

Dynasty. Gilles de Rais is a French nobleman from the 15th century who grow to be accused of killing over

a hundred years later. We discover some of psychoopathic killers the numerous Ripper's contemporaries. These encompass serial poisoner Mary Ann Cotton and Jane Toppan (and Chicago's "Torture Doctor" Dr. H.H. Holmes.

Jack became now not the primary. We can thoroughly say that Whitechapel's serial killer has attracted extra morbid hobby than some distinct serial killer. There are few historical figures that have acquired as many manuscripts, from non-fiction works to doctoral-nice scholarly works, than Whitechapel. There have moreover been TV specials, movies, television suggests, comedian books and themed walks. Even an opera. Recently, net chatrooms and net web sites have emerged wherein Ripper fanatics can talk their favored theories to their coronary coronary heart's content material fabric.

Why is this example so important?

It's the conventional homicide thriller. The fog is full of a fiend, who takes sufferers as he pleases, and his bloodlust escalates with each new crime. After a totally remaining act of fantastic violence, he disappears. We are left to surprise who he is, what motivated him, and why he stopped . This has all the factors that make a extraordinary whodunit except that we do now not have Sherlock Holmes or Hercule poirot to help us find out the killer.

Will we ever find out Jack's actual identity? Unfortunately, no. Although many names have been suggested, none of them in form the bill.

However, we do now not recognize the whole thing approximately the Ripper. Through eyewitness testimony, we have got an remarkable concept of his look; thru examination of the crimes, we are able to form a sturdy image about his reasons and man or woman. Criminal psychologists can also assist us to understand his motivations and person. Pathology evaluations offer insight into his mode of operation and solution the essential query whether or not or now not or not he obtained medical schooling.

We understand masses about Jack the Ripper, however the thriller surrounding the case. It is genuinely that we are not able to perceive him.

We haven't given up on attempting. Over the years, endless authors tried to persuade us that the Ripper emerge as absolutely a person else. The theories furnished with the useful resource of these authors are often unfounded and at instances quite absurd. The Ripper end up a murderous cotton carrier business enterprise, he became a famous painter, and he grow to be the inheritor of the British throne. None of these claims are proper, lamentably. They are in reality the end result of twisting records and digging up "evidence" to aid a domestic dog concept. This isn't the approach I will take in this book.

Instead, I is probably revisiting the times, inspecting the credentials of the suspects cited, and dispelling not unusual myths. I will be reviewing the proof and calling upon the help of professional profilers to create a photograph approximately the maximum mysterious killer in statistics. If this sounds thrilling, I invite you to join me on an exploration into one of the finest mysteries of the area.

We'll first want to observe inside the footsteps the Ripper. Allow me to take you on a frightening adventure of the mind decrease decrease returned to London's East End, on a cold, moist August 1888.

Murder Most Foul

Mary Ann Nichols' Unquiet Death

Polly Nicholls modified right into a underneath the affect of alcohol. This turned into common. Polly become like a number of the 1,200 prostitutes in London's East End. She had no awesome pursuits than a regular glass of reasonably-priced gin. Whitechapel's whoring industrial agency became tough, and uncovered its humans to violence and disease. It fee fine three pence in line with hour. As it have become out, three pence became the charge of one shot of Gin. Polly did not hold the cash prolonged in her wallet earlier than she exceeded it over to the publican on the neighborhood tavern.

Polly became consuming as loads as she may also want to at the bloodless, drizzly night time of August 30, 1888. She left the Frying Pan Pub on Brick Lane at round 12:20 on Friday, August 31 and made her way to her resorts residence at 18 Thrawl Street. Polly didn't hesitate to pay 4 pence for a single bed, but she wasn't going to prevent her from paying the relaxation. Polly have emerge as ejected from her room at 1:forty a.M. After unsuccessful negotiations with the deputy of the boarding house.

It did no longer appear to problem her the least bit. She come to be brimming with gin, and she or he or he appeared to be in a glad mood. She stated, "I'll speedy get my doss coins," and did a little pirouette. She said, "See how jolly I am." And she grow to be out the door.

It have been raining intermittently all day and Polly changed into leaving the boardinghouse whilst it began out to drizzle. A nearby Shadwell Dry Dock have become lit through a blaze, which solid a unusual reddish glow at the cloud. This turned into in all likelihood a sign of the destiny.

Polly met Emily Holland on Whitechapel Road at round 2:30. Polly declined Emily's offer of a mattress in her room for the night, and said that she may pay her way. She stated, "I actually have had my doss coins three greater times today and I've spent it." She said, "It gained't be lengthy until I'm decrease once more." And then she stumbled off, heading East. This modified into the ultimate time simply every body, except her killer, noticed Polly alive.

Charles Cross, someone who became walking along Buck's Row that morning at four o'clock in the morning, observed a few element on the floor. He notion it regarded like a discarded canvas, however closer inspection determined out that it modified into genuinely a girl mendacity on her stomach, her skirts extending to her waist. Cross notion she come to be below the have an effect on of alcohol or had been assaulted. He known as Robert Paul, a passerby. They went collectively to the female's resource.

Cross reduced right into a crouch and approached the body with warning. The fingers of the lady have been very bloodless and limp. He informed his companion, "I receive as genuine with that she is lifeless." Paul completed his non-public assessment by way of the usage of manner of setting his ear on the woman's chest. He said that he believed she have emerge as respiration. But handiest just.

The guys took off the ladies's skirts and walked off to find out a policeman. The avenue changed into darkish and gloomy, with handiest a single fuel lamp a distance away, so neither man located Polly Nichols' terrible accidents to her throat. They nearly needed to decapitate her.

Mary Ann Nichols

Cross and Paul met PC Mizen at Old Hanbury a short time later.

Street, and shared what they observed. Mizen short set out inside the direction of Buck's Row. Constable John Neil, every different officer, determined the frame by the time Mizen arrived. Neil examined the horrendous scene together along together with his lantern. The female's eyes were open and blood changed into seeping from her throat. Neil became regardless of the fact that baffled as to why there wasn't extra. This scene need to have been saturated with the stuff. Another peculiarity become positioned. The corpse's hands, decrease fingers, and better arms had been bloodless but the pinnacle arms had been nonetheless warm. Polly changed into no longer dead for prolonged. Cross and Paul probable sincerely disregarded out on catching her killer.

Neil right now sent PC Thain to the scene to get Dr. Llewellyn, a neighborhood constable. Mizen grow to be dispatched to name for backup at the nearby Bethnal Green Police Station. Another officer, Sergeant. Sgt. Kirby, arrived and started knocking on doors to wake people up from their sleep. However, no person had seen or heard a few thing. It modified into nearly as though Polly Nichols were killed thru a ghost.

Dr. Rees Llewellyn arrived on the scene truely in advance than four o'clock. Dr. Rees Llewellyn rapid tested the woman and anticipated that she were lifeless for much less than half of an hour. Two deep slashes to her throat and all of the way to her spinal column had been the reason of her loss of lifestyles. They had cut the windpipe and esophagus so deeply that they had been unable to breathe.

A huge crowd of commuters in the early morning had already started out out to attain, pressing ahead to appearance the scary scene. Dr. Llewellyn suggested that the frame have come to be taken to Old Montague Street's mortuary. In any occasion, he had finished his examination. Or so he concept.

Officers Neil, Mizen and Kirby determined a corpse on the fast enjoy to the morgue. PC Thain remained at the scene to look at for Inspector John Spratling's arrival. The inspector arrived to locate that the crime scene became wiped easy up and the blood had been washed a long way from the frame via way of a close-by boy. After a brief inspection of the vicinity, he concluded that not some thing have emerge as of any import. He then headed to the mortuary to study the corpse. He reached for the lady's skirt, and located a beautiful discovery that the health practitioner and one-of-a-kind officers had unnoticed. The killer had no longer most effective reduce Polly's throat, but moreover ripped her stomach open. The jagged reduce ran nearly from the breastbone to the pubic bone. It turn out to be so deep that the girl's intestines were uncovered. The telephone rang unexpectedly after.

Dr. Llewellyn's home jangled into existence, and he grow to be summoned at the mortuary.

Second examination found that the stomach wound changed into postmortem. The thriller surrounding the shortage of blood turned into moreover solved. There have become a few bruising inside the neck and jaw, further to round contusions on either aspect of the throat which appeared to be thumb impressions. This indicated that the woman come to be overwhelmed into submission and then lessen. It is feasible that she turn out to be even strangled to demise. This need to offer an motive behind why there wasn't a surge of blood from each the carotid or jugular veins. Dr. Llewellyn believed she have been mendacity down while the knife wounds had been made. This induced blood to float down her neck and pool beneath her, with an lousy lot of it being absorbed with the aid of her garb layers. The medical doctor subsequently discovered that the cuts were inflicted on her left hand. He may additionally later trade his thoughts. The legend of Jack the Ripper being left-handed although lives directly to in recent times.

The autopsy record allowed the police to form a concept regarding the conditions of the murder. The police believed the killer had strangled the victim alongside alongside with his palms, either killing him or rendering her unconscious. The killer then slashed her instances for the duration of her throat in advance than putting her at the ground. His blade pierced the victim's spine. He continued to lust after blood and lifted the woman's skirt before ripping open her stomach. Although his cause grow to be to inflict greater atrocities, he had been disturbed through Charles Cross's arrival and fled.

Investigators had to locate the sufferer, which modified into hard even as she high-quality had a comb, damaged mirror and a handkerchief. The police placed that a lady known as "Polly" turn out to be lacking from her 18thrawl Street lodges because the information of the murder spread in some unspecified time inside the destiny of Whitechapel. Mary Ann Nichols, forty two, modified into the real "Polly". The subsequent day, her father and husband identified her.

Polly became married to William Nichols. They had 5 kids together. Due to her drinking, their marriage have grow to be broken and Polly had drifted into prostitution. She provided herself on the streets for a small quantity that she quick spent on booze at the neighborhood tavern. It modified into a depressing life that caused a tragic surrender.

Inspector became appointed to investigate the murder of Polly Nicholls.

Joseph Helson was the pinnacle of CID inside the J or Bethnal Green Division in which the body became placed. Helson right away started walking and dispatched officers to go searching the streets, alongside nearby rail traces. They looked for proof of the assassin's break out path, a weapon, or a blood route. Although the search changed into exhaustive, no longer something end up placed.

Officers knocked on doors to inquire about the citizens become some other street. Despite the truth Polly Nicholls' lack of life being truly toes from severa houses, officials knocked on doors to inquire about the citizens.

Chapter 8: The Internet Net Page Of Nichols Murder

Abberline Takes Charge

While the studies grow to be ongoing, there was each different critical improvement Scotland Yard decided to sign up within the research, and taken in their personal guy to supervise the efforts of severa divisional commanders. It changed into Chief Inspector Frederick George Abberline who could be inextricably connected to the case. The Whitechapel murders had been a thriller that no one-of-a-kind officer needs to have exposed. Abberline, aside from Jack, is the maximum carefully related personage with the case.

Chief Inspector Frederick Abberline

Abberline, a 25-12 months veteran of police, modified into on the Ripper studies. 14 years of that element had been spent in Whitechapel. His face modified into included in a bushy mustache, and his element whiskers were in addition furry. He modified into 45 years of age, weighed over 100 45 and bald. Abberline grow to be a remarkable investigator with a stellar document of arrests. Abberline changed into as a substitute valid via using his superiors and co-people. He come to be additionally cherished via the community that he worked with. As a token of understand and appreciation, Abberline emerge as furnished with an eye constant made from gold with the useful resource of Whitechapel, Spitalfields, and Spitalfields upon his transfer to Scotland Yard.

You may surprise why the Metropolitan Police had assigned this type of senior officer for a easy murder of a prostitute. Polly Nicholls wasn't the handiest prostitute brutally murdered in East End currently. Despite the hardships and random violence that have been a part of ghetto living, homicide changed into unusual. But, Polly's lack of life brought to a few the range unsolved murders of streetwalkers.

Martha Tabram, a robust female, grow to be gift on Monday, August 6, 1888.

Built prostitute in her past due thirties. She have been asking for alternate on. Whitechapel Road, with Mary Ann Connolly (regionally called "Pearly Poll"), a few one of a kind streetwalker.

They ended up forming a friendship with guardsmen, one corporal and one private. After some time, they cherished some beverages in precise pubs alongside Whitechapel Road. They paired up at spherical 11:30. Martha disappeared with one soldier within the George Yard darkened thoroughfare, even as Pearly poll led the opportunity to a close-by area.

Martha used George Yard regularly for short sex liaisons, acknowledged colloquially with the resource of "4-penny tremblers" She led the soldier from this region.

Joseph and Elizabeth Mahoney, who had celebrated the Bank Holiday collectively with their buddies, returned to George Yard homes inside the early hours of the morning. Elizabeth then went to Thrawl Street to get dinner at a close-by chandler's. Nothing come to be untoward as she climbed and diminished the darkened staircase.

Alfred George Crow, a taxi driving force, again from artwork at spherical 3 o'clock within the morning. He changed into mountain climbing up the steps whilst he located someone sound asleep on the number one floor touchdown. It wasn't uncommon for vagrants to sleep on landings.

John Saunders Reeves, a dock worker, left George Yard Buildings truely after five a.M. To visit art work. Reeves additionally observed the frame on the floor however it changed into turning into slight. Reeves ought to see the pool of blood throughout the inclined body, which Crow had no longer seen. Reeves raced to find a cop and grow to be soon greeted with the useful resource of Constable T. Barrett at George Yard.

Barrett brief discovered that the girl had died. While he watched the corpse, he dispatched Reeves to Dr. Killeen's nearby residence. After a short examination, the doctor declared the lady's lack of life, steady together with his opinion, because of being brutally murdered. Killeen's testimony on the inquest later might verify the brutality of the assault. The sufferer sustained 39 knife accidents, the bulk of which were because of an normal clasp knife, but as a minimum one have become because of an extended-bladed device, likely a bayonet.

The crime become first investigated with the useful resource of the usage of George Collier, deputy coroner. He defined it as "surely certainly one of maximum horrible murders all of us should believe." However, this lead brief dissolved and the case remained unsolved.

Another unsolved murder of a prostitute had taken area a few months earlier than.

April 2, 1888. Emma, forty five years vintage, have become decided within the early hours of the morning.

Smith changed into brutally attacked through the use of three guys from the Osborn Street and Wentworth Street intersections. This is honestly 100 yards far from Martha Tabram's corpse. Emma have grow to be problem to a brutal beating, and then she have emerge as raped through a fixed of 3 men earlier than a blunt object, perhaps a stick modified into pressured into her genitals. After robbing Emma of the pennies she had in her pocket, they fled.

Emma Smith survived the attack and turned into in a function to stroll decrease decrease again to her home. Several residents glad her to go to the London Hospital Whitechapel Road. She knowledgeable her story to the docs. Her injuries had been so excessive that she died tomorrow. The police have been not informed about the murder till April 6. The verdict of the inquest changed into "Wilful Murder in the direction of unknown people".

Whitechapel citizens believed Tabram and Smith's attacks were the result of the same guy who killed Polly Nichols. This is honestly no longer real inside the case Emma Smith. Smith became attacked by way of severa men and certainly the motive was rape and robbery. It is apparent that the attackers did not intend to homicide, irrespective of the brutality and violence of the attack. Smith said that the men had been consuming. It is feasible that they took their attack to a ways.

Martha Tabram, but? It is feasible that Martha Tabram became the victim of the identical murderer as Polly Nichols. The murders seem very top notch. Martha turned into again and again stabbed, but now not mutilated. Polly was now not stabbed, however her throat become lessen and she or he also obtained autopsy accidents. This isn't unusual in serial murder times. The killer stays seeking to determine out his manner with the primary murder. He is greater assured and able to inflict the ones accidents that he has lengthy fantasized about. It's viable that Martha Tabram emerge as Jack the Rifle's first sufferer. Experts at the Ripper are divided approximately this problem.

Martha Tabram

Chapter 9: The Man Within The Leather Apron

It is essential to recognise the history of the Whitechapel murders a awesome way to certainly understand them. One not unusual misconception about the generation is that it end up all one large, filthy slum in the East End, populated with the aid of a criminal and immoral underclass, one step away from savages. This is honestly fake. Although the vicinity have turn out to be terrible, it became populated thru hardworking, first rate, honest people. It have become no worse than the slums of other extra upscale London neighborhoods like Chelsea, Westminster or even the City.

However, there had been a few areas inside the East End that the stereotype was true. One of these become the square mile in which the Ripper murders happened. It was a place wherein loads of human beings lived in crumbling tenements. This have turn out to be wherein sheep and cattle have been moved through slim streets to the slaughterhouses. The air turn out to be thickened with the odor of liquid sewage, rotting rubbish and the stench from the abattoirs. Many of the residents lived in horrible conditions. Some were compelled to live in hotels that fee between and four kilos steady with night time time. A bunk became 4 pence. Two pence must get you a bunk. Over half of those born into this poverty died in advance than they had been five years vintage. Many of folks who survived were mentally or physically handicapped.

The majority of East End residents at some point of this era were hired in menial jobs, but many had been furthermore unemployed or subsisted by means of way of severa criminal businesses. There grow to be an lousy lot much less opportunity for East End women. They had few different dependable tactics to make a dwelling. Prostitution changed into one manner. Whitechapel's 1888 census located the massive sort of prostitutes at 1,two hundred. This excludes girls who whore on occasion to supplement their meager incomes.

This vicinity become acknowledged for its poverty, crime, squalor, and crowded tenements. There were moreover narrow darkened streets and alleyways that delivered approximately the regions wherein girls in decided situations had to assignment out on the streets at night time time to earn a residing. This vicinity modified into the right hunting ground for an enterprising serial murderer.

Yet, homicide became no longer commonplace even below those instances. It turn out to be a stunning incident, specially thinking about that maximum humans believed that Tabram, Smith and Nichols had been all devoted by the same man. This worry changed into amplified with the aid of manner of the media, which alternately noted recollections about a crook gang preying on prostitutes or a homicidal lunatic stalking the streets searching out prey. Although plenty of those tales have been later confirmed to be fake, it did now not prevent the panic. Whitechapel changed into dominated by way of the murders. Women shuddered at the notion that a knife-wielding fend is probably looking earlier to them virtually across the nook. The spot in which Polly Nichols modified into killed have come to be a type of shrine. This attracted hordes upon hordes morbid interest seekers, who sat silently whispering in reverent tones as people who claimed to be informed talked about the right region.

The day of Polly's funeral, September 6, 1888 located a big crowd collect in the the front of the Old Montague Street morgue. Police officials had been known as in to smooth the path for the hearse to leave the premises. As the procession headed to Ilford's City of London Cemetery, Polly may be laid in kingdom. Crowds amassed alongside the streets. It have emerge as nearly as even though the whole network turned into grieving together.

A community provider issuer wrote a letter to Henry Matthews, the Home Secretary, asking him to offer a praise to capture the killer. Matthews declined, pointing out that it turned into no longer government coverage. He moreover reiterated his belief within the Metropolitan Police's functionality to capture the criminal.

This belief became confirmed with the resource of manner of detectives who diagnosed John Pizer, a Polish Jew, because of the reality the suspect inside the Nicholls' homicide. Pizer grow to be locally referred to as "Leather Apron" and had a reputation for extorting coins from prostitutes. He additionally beat them inside the event that they refused. Pizer have turn out to be described as five-foot 4, with a thick neck and heavyset. His eyes were small and glistening, and his lips parted in a menacing smile. His hair have turn out to be black and tightly cropped. His nickname end up derived from his small, black moustache, which he wore with a black, leather-based-based totally-based totally apron.

Leather Apron turn out to be as quickly as a slipper-maker, but he had seemingly given up that alternate to make it less complicated for the easy coins. His motto changed into simplicity. His M.O. Became simplicity. He may also usually wait outdoor taverns till the morning, hoping for a prostitute to come back returned by myself. He should then comply with the lady along a darkened road, wherein he ought to sneak up on her and take keep of her throat. According to his patients, he modified into a grasp of stealth. A razorsharp knife made of leather-based became additionally reportedly on his waist. This is a remnant from his former profession.

This made "Leather Aprilon" a very feasible suspect within the Whitechapel crime. However, it proved difficult to locate him. It end up even greater tough at the same time as the newspapers had been given wind of the story, and started walking articles that each one however diagnosed Pizer as Whitechapel's killer. The suspect fled to cover alongside along with his family, fearing mob justice. When the Ripper took a few other victim, he turn out to be however at large.

Lightning Strikes Again

The Murder of Dark Annie Chapman

Annie Chapman changed into as speedy as a reputable, married mom of three kids. After her 12th birthday, her oldest little one died from meningitis, Annie and John began out to drink. This caused their eventual divorce. Annie end up left with little to no assist after John's loss of existence. She suffered from melancholy and alcoholism and come to be left without any help. So she became to prostitution. She modified into 47 years vintage and notwithstanding the reality that labored the streets. A sad, damaged lady, her life have become on the verge of completing.

Annie modified right right into a standout maximum of the East End's streetwalkers.

She became in reality over 5 ft tall and had a dark complexion, thick nose, and pallid pores and skin. Her pinnacle the the the front enamel have been lacking. Despite her appearance being unattractive, she become a candy, annoying soul who modified into nicely-desired with the aid of all and tough jogging whilst she wasn't eating. She changed into not excellent a prostitute, but furthermore made artificial vegetation and crocheted for income.

Ted Staley have become certainly one in every of Annie's ordinary clients. He might probable spend weekends with Annie. Staley, who modified into diagnosed to Annie's lodgers as "the Pensioner", seemed to be very controlling over Annie. He had as soon as warned her lodges house deputy to no longer permit Annie to deliver one-of-a-type men to the house. She emerge as also concerned in the pleasant altercation that anyone observed.

Annie borrowed a bar cleaning cleaning soap from Eliza Cooper to apply for Staley. This changed into the concept of their argument. Cooper and Annie had a heated trade at the equal time as Annie failed to move returned her bar on time. A few days later, Annie appeared wearing severa bruises, which encompass a black eye.

Although the injuries have been not excessive, Annie Chapman's behavior became. In the final days of her existence she seemed listless and changed into honestly in ache. Amelia Parker, a chum of hers, informed her three days in advance than her demise that she had taken into consideration going to the health center to get treatment.

She confided to Parker that she didn't have enough coins for food because of the reality she become now not succesful art work. Parker gave her pence so she could buy meals, however warned her inside the course of spending the coins on alcohol. Annie regarded slightly higher while she observed her on September 7. She said, "It's no longer well actually really worth giving up." Annie Chapman's final terms to Amelia were "I need to get myself together and get some cash or I will have no hotels.".

Annie arrived at her accommodations house on 35 Dorset Street at 7:15 p.M. That night time time and asked Timothy Donovan, the deputy, if she would like to sit within the kitchen. Annie stayed there till nighttime, at the same time as Donovan sent John Evans, the night time watchman to invite for cash for her bed. Annie stated that she didn't have any coins because of the truth she had spent the beyond few days inside the clinic. Then, she went to Donovan's place of work to try to convince him to allow her stay for the night time time. Donovan changed into able to see that Annie have been eating, and he declined to allow her live the night time time. He stated, "If you could find the money for beer, you may have sufficient cash to shop for a mattress.".

Annie want to have decided out that it end up futile to argue the point further. She have come to be and left, telling Donovan to make certain she had a bed for her. John Evans became close by as she walked towards the door. She said, "It won't be extended earlier than you're in," He watched as she hurried closer to Little Paternoster Row, then became right into Brushfield Street. He later told investigators that she became "a bit tipsy", but not drunk.

We lose tune of Dark Annie's area over the subsequent 3 hours. According to at the least one witness, she end up visible within the Ten Bells Pub from five a.M.

Until she left with someone sporting "a bit cranium cap". This sighting has never been showed. We do understand that Annie have become in Spitalfields on Hanbury Street at 5:30 a.M., just a few steps from the Ten Bells.

Hanbury Street changed into included along every facets via 4-story, foreboding homes. Each of those houses have been divided into small residential devices and allow to character or complete households. These narrow passageways ran along the period of the constructing from the the the the front doors to the steps important to the better flooring to the door putting in to the over again. Many residents worked at Spitalfields Market, in order that they regularly left early for paintings and lower lower lower back past due. This intended that the doors to the houses' the the front doors have been frequently left unlocked. Local prostitutes were well privy to this and used it to their advantage. They could often take their clients via the long passageways to the again yards of Hanbury Street homes. Sometimes they might now not trouble to transport that some distance, and may finish the transaction in one of the landings or the hallways.

The everyday residence that covered the road have become 29 Hanbury Street. The tenement housed 17 people in eight rooms. A basement have come to be home to a packing case corporation, owned with the useful resource of Mrs. Amelia Richardson. On Saturday, September 8, John have emerge as wakeful amongst 4:40 and four:45 AM.

Richardson known as the residence on the equal time as he end up on his manner to artwork. He got here to examine the cellar door which allowed him to get right of access to his mom's enterprise. One month in advance, someone had damaged into the padlock. John has been checking at the premises periodically because of the fact then to ensure the whole lot is so as.

He became carrying new boots which have been too tight in this morning. He felt one of the boots pinch his toe, so he went to the again stairs and reduce a bit of leather the use of a desk knife. He may additionally additionally need to appearance the padlock intact while he sat on the second one step. He did no longer see a few aspect else uncommon in his yard. He become completed with the shoe repair and he continued his adventure.

Mrs. Elizabeth Long, who grow to be on her manner to Spitalfields Market at 5:30 am, passed someone with a girl out of doors variety 29 as she walked alongside Hanbury Street. Although she couldn't see his face, she later described him as being spherical 40 years of age, with dark pores and skin and "overseas looking." His look was not a terrific deal specific from the female's and featured a dark overcoat, brown deerstalker hat, and grow to be no longer an awful lot shorter than hers. However, Mrs. Long emerge as insistent approximately the identification. Annie Chapman was the female. She surpassed the individual and he asked, "Will your partner marry me?" The lady replied, "Yes."

Albert Cadoche (a wood employee who lived proper subsequent to Cadoche at range 27), walked into his outdoor a quick time later. He stood there and heard one phrase discovering the fence. It have come to be a girl's voice announcing "No." Cadoche went in however decrease again to his outside three mins later. He idea he heard some factor falling against the fence that separated his assets from variety 29.

He didn't count on an entire lot of it on the time and shortly after, he have become off to paintings. He emerge as walking along Commercial Street when he noticed the clock at Christchurch Spitalfields. It changed into 5:32 AM.

John Davis, an elderly carman, rented an attic place at 29 Hanbury. Davis came all the manner right all the way down to the basement at 6 AM. He walked thru the narrow passageway, after which opened the door main out to the out of doors. Davis proper away stumbled once more in horror and almost fell earlier than he regained his stability. Davis ran down the passage, stumbling and almost falling before he grow to be able to stability himself. He then opened the door that led out onto the street. He observed two guys, James Kent, and Henry Holland. He demanded that they come to him. The men followed him into the house, down the darkened hallway and returned to his room.

Annie Chapman lay at the ground a few of the stairs of the wooden fence and her head changed into grew to grow to be closer to the residence. Her skirts have been pulled as an entire lot as her waist, exposing her pink-and-white striped stockings. Her legs have been drawn up together with her toes at the ground, and her knees have become outwards. All of this modified into trivial in evaluation to the horrific mutilations she had suffered. Her face became swelling together along with her tongue protruding among her the the front teeth. The viscera were pulled via her belly to the top of the right shoulder. The stomach end up in part removed and lay on pinnacle of her left shoulder. The throat modified into badly slit and there has been loads of blood on the ground.

After absorbing the bleak scene for a few seconds, they raced off to find out a policeman. James Kent become so shaken by means of the use of manner of the sight that he abandoned his look for a policeman and went to a neighborhood pub to get a huge brandy. Henry Holland had, but, run to Spitalfields Market to tell a constable who turn out to be on sentry duty. The bobby refused his assistance and stated that he wasn't allowed to depart his position.

John Davis, an elderly carman, emerge as the best who subsequently controlled to summon assist. He have become already heading right away to Commercial Street Police Station, and he demanded to talk with the officer in charge. Soon Inspector Joseph Chandler was rushing in the direction of the scene.

Chapter 10: Annie Chapman

Chandler arrived genuinely in time to discover that there were every other

murder. There became already a big crowd outside of 29 Hanbury. Some had even attempted to enter the house. Chandler quick referred to as for reinforcements to clean the vicinity of sight-seekers. The Divisional Police Surgeon, Dr. George Bagster Phillips come to be then dispatched.

Dr. Phillips arrived at the scene round 6:30 AM. By that point, the group out of doors had grown to severa hundred. After a cursory inspection of the victim's frame, Phillips determined out that he come to be unable to provide clinical help and began out a forensic exam.

Phillips concluded that the lady modified into dead for at least two hours, and that she had likely been strangled with postmortem mutilations. Phillips' conclusion about the time of loss of life is inconsistent with Albert Cadoche's and Elizabeth Long's witness statements. It is sort of effective that this is inaccurate. All proof shows that Annie Chapman changed into murdered round 5:30 a.M.

How should Dr. Phillips, a seasoned police pathologist, make this error? His assessment must have relied particularly at the sufferer's body temperature and rigor mortis. It appears that he did no longer hold in mind the take a seat lower again of the morning, the reality that the sufferer grow to be open and had professional giant blood loss. These elements should have prompted speedy warmth loss within the corpse.

This mistakes apart, Dr. Phillip's exam gave an intensive, however scary, account of the corpse. Annie Chapman come to be strangled, it's far smooth. She had thumb marks and scratches on her throat that proved this. However, her loss of lifestyles could have been due to blood loss from the deep slashes to her throat. The evidence that her throat changed into slitted suggests that she changed into probable aware, but there was an boom in blood strain towards the fence.

Dr. Phillips furnished extra testimony at the inquest concerning the brutality and severity of the crime. Annie emerge as slashed from the left to the right via her murderer. Although he also can have tried to kill Annie, the laceration have come to be immoderate and sufficient to motive her loss of lifestyles. These have been the information of the belly mutilations:

The stomach emerge as in reality open. The intestines had been eliminated from their mesenteric attachments and lifted from the body. The pelvis had furthermore been empty. These components had been no longer discovered. The incisions have been made cleanly, with out causing any harm to the cervix. Evidently, this modified into the artwork of an expert, or at least one that had lots records approximately anatomical and pathological examinations that he should stable the pelvic organs using one stroke of the knife.

Phillips stated that the operation changed into to attain the frame elements. He modified into amazed that such professional cuts can be made on this form of quick amount of time. He stated that a 23-year-antique health practitioner may have required fifteen minutes minimum and much more likely an hour to finish the cuts.

In his summation, Coroner Wynne Baxter stated that he believed that the wrongdoer end up a person with "massive records and anatomical capabilities."

Other proof turn out to be moreover positioned at the scene. The useless female had bruises and abrasions on her fingers, which counseled that jewelry were forcibly removed.

Annie's pal should later verify that she wore brass jewelry. They were possibly taken through manner of the killer and in no way observed.

An array of objects have end up located within the victim's pocket, along with a square of coarse-muslin, scissors, and an envelope with some tablets. The objects were prepared deliberately by the usage of the victim's feet. Detectives could not determine why the killer did this, however they were able to grow to be aware of the purpose. It have become perception that the murderer may additionally were connected to freemasonry. Inspector Joseph Chandler, of the Metropolitan Police's H Division come to be given charge of the Annie Chapman homicide studies. Inspector Abberline changed into his overseer. Evidently, the Met's top brass believed that the murderer become the equal man who killed Polly Nicholls.

The research into Chapman's murder of Nicholls changed into a comparable one. However, it quick have emerge as obstructed through a lack of evidence. The killer took a wonderful chance thru the usage of committing the crime at daytime right next to the Spitalfields Market. The killer had then left the scene and walked away, likely protected in blood and carrying the organs he had simply harvested. Yet, no witnesses had been able to be located who may additionally need to have visible some thing or all and sundry else.

Although the investigators had some leads, the maximum critical clues supplied by using witnesses Richardson and Long had been with the aid of and massive not noted as they conflicted with the coroner's time of lack of existence. There is a possibility that Elizabeth Long may have visible someone matching those descriptions if those leads have been determined. He might have been wearing a suspicious-searching parcel, wrapped in bloody paper.

Yard at 29 Hanbury Street, in which Annie Chapman have grow to be murdered

Panic in Whitechapel

The Aftermath of Chapman Murder

Annie Chapman's homicide, so close to the brutal killings

Polly Nicholls, and Martha Tabram stable worry and suspicion on the East End. A organization of nearby businessmen shaped the Mile End Vigilance Committee to counter the growing anti-Semitic sentiment. It modified right into a form of community watch below the direction of George Lusk (a nearby contractor). Lusk's committee wasn't the excellent one to emerge in the wake the Ripper murders. However, it turn out to be the most well-known due to the "Dear Boss", a letter purportedly written with the aid of the killer and addressed to Lusk.

sixteen nearby traders, regularly of Jewish historic past, common the Committee. Its number one desires have been to gather coins for a reward, and to distribute flyers looking for information. Later, it might come to be a club.

"community watch" patrols. The committee did not acquire its most critical intention, and it have become obvious brief. While Whitechapel citizens applauded Lusk for his efforts, they weren't prepared to make a contribution to a reward fund on the same time as their government refused to.

Lusk answered via attractive right now to Queen Victoria.

The Home Secretary's Office intercepted the letter and Lusk have come to be given a quick reply reiterating the government's previous function. Although the police were decided to make a brief arrest, there was no praise. Joseph Aarons, Vigilance Committee secretary wrote an open letter addressed to Henry Matthews, Home Secretary, in protest at this refusal. Aarons asked the authorities why it had furnished a bounty to Lord Cavendish's assassins, however refused to "avenge the ones unlucky women's blood." Matthews did no longer respond, however Samuel Montagu, Jewish Member of Parliament, for Whitechapel, did. He supplied a praise. It did now not produce any tangible results.

Mr. George Lusk

John Pizer, additionally known as the "Leather Apron," have grow to be arrested on Tuesday, 9-11, just a few days following the murder of Annie Chapman. The police knew from the begin that Pizer come to be no longer the Whitechapel killer. Although he become gifted with a leather-based-primarily based knife he did now not own the surgical skills and anatomical understanding Dr. Phillips believed he had. Pizer turn out to be furthermore able to supply strong alibis for each homicide. Although he emerge as a rather unsightly person, Pizer is most truely now not Jack the Ripper. He modified into quickly freed.

There have been many special arrests that decided. These were generally drunks who were enthralled via the murders and then tried to interrupt out with it. They have been not held for lengthy.

It changed into difficult to discover an area in Whitechapel without hearing approximately the murders at that time. People spoke quietly about the monster dwelling of their midst in muffled tones. There had been many wild rumors. There had been many rumors. One was that every other mutilated corpse had been determined, this time in the place of London Hospital. Another perception changed into that a message had written on the door at 29, Hanbury Street. It have end up said, "This is the fourth." "I will kill 16 human beings and then surrender on myself."

Reports additionally referred to suspects, generally villainous-looking guys, who appeared in some manner just like the guy Mrs. Long saw. However, one sighting is absolutely nicely really worth mentioning. Mrs. Fiddymont was the partner and owner of Prince Albert pub on the intersection of Stewart Streets and Brushfield Streets. A guy approached the pub in the early hours of the Chapman homicide and requested half of of a pint. While Mrs. Fiddymont changed into drawing her pint, the individual seemed in the bar mirror. He changed into center-elderly, medium in pinnacle, had quick sandy hair, and had a ginger moustache. Mrs. Fiddymont determined that there has been a small quantity of blood below his right ear, and that there were specks of the stuff among his palms and his right hand. He speedy finished the beer as brief as he noticed Mrs. Fiddymont.

Joseph Taylor, a pub customer, observed the man or woman's bizarre conduct and moreover positioned it. He determined to comply with the man to Half Moon Street in Bishopsgate, but he lost him within the crowd. Later, he stated that the man or woman appeared demanding and disoriented with staring eyes and wild expressions. The Prince Albert become positioned just 400 meters from the crime scene. Police had been interested by the report but got here up empty. In connection to every other Ripper murder, the character with the ginger moustache is probably referred to.

These critiques, together with the frequently reckless reporting of the newspapers, helped to infuse the East End with a palpable feeling of panic. The streets have been almost deserted except for the patrolling bobbies, at the same time as darkness introduced an unofficial curfew. Even despite the fact that there was a homicidal lunac, Whitechapel's raucous nightlife did now not prevent. It have become crucial for the livelihoods of many.

Just as topics were beginning to normalize, each other terrible improvement came about. It may additionally have a profound impact at the case, and Ripper folklore. A letter arrived at Central News Agency offices on September 27, 1888. It changed into written in crimson ink and reads as follows:

25 Sept 1888

Dear Boss

I preserve listening to that the police have arrested me, but they won't be capable of restore me but. I've laughed at their cleverness and boasting approximately being on the proper path. I changed into absolutely enraged through the comic tale approximately Leather Apron. I'm a slob and could maintain to rip them until I get buckled. The final job modified right into a exceptional one. The girl grow to be a whimpering break. I do not know how they could trap me now. I love what I do and would love to retain. My funny video games will soon be remembered. Over the very last interest, I had a few crimson ink stored in a ginger beer glass. But it have come to be too thick and I can't use it. I'm tremendous purple ink might be quality. Clipping might be my next interest. You can take the girl's ears and ship it to the Police officials for a few jolly, would now not you? This letter need to be saved another time till I actually have completed a few more artwork earlier than I deliver it to you. My knife is so sharp and remarkable that I want to proper away get to artwork if I definitely have the risk.

Good true fortune.

Yours absolutely

Jack the Ripper

I'm satisfactory with you giving the change name

The Ripper legend has blanketed this letter and each other that come to be sent to George Lusk, Mile End Vigilance Committee, nearly three weeks later. Today, you could not find out any Ripper expert who believes they are right. Their origins have been doubtful even again then. They did but gain one component: they gave Whitechapel's murderer his frightening nom de guerre.

Chapter 11: The Murder Of Long Liz Stride

Although the "Dear Boss", letter might have been a hoax, the warning that it contained: "I love and need to preserve my artwork" have emerge as out to be a sign of what emerge as to move again. Three days after the letter arrived, the Ripper struck all over again. This time, he claimed victims in a single night time.

Elizabeth Stride, additionally called "Long Liz", come to be a Swedish immigrant who worked in a family as a servant. Sometimes she supplemented her meager profits through way of prostitution. Elizabeth worked in a inns house cleansing rooms for sixpence on her closing day. She changed into ingesting her income at Queen's Head, nook Fashion and Commercial Streets, with the useful resource of 6:30 p.M. She later again to her resorts at spherical 7:30, dressed "for a nighttime out," consistent with one in every of her fellow citizens.

Elizabeth changed into subsequent seen at 11 o'clock, at the same time as she have become seen sheltering from the downpour inside the the the front of Bricklayer's Arms pub on Settles Street. She wasn't the handiest one there. She became not the high-quality one. There became moreover a person around five' five" tall, with a black moustache and wearing a first rate black morning healthy. The guy and he or she have been in passionate encompass. Gardner and Best, passersby, couldn't resist mocking the couple. Best exclaimed, "Watch out! That's Leather Apron getting spherical you!" The couple ran into the rain and headed closer to Commercial Road.

Elizabeth Stride and her guy want to have parted methods fast, as she changed into found round

eleven:45 p.M. A laborer named William Marshall noticed her outdoor variety sixty three Berner Street with a few different man. The guy changed into center-aged, nicely-constructed, and easy-shaven. Marshall heard the person tell the lady, "You could now not say a few thing besides your prayers," earlier than they walked away within the direction of Dutfield's yard.

PC William Smith, a walker on Berner Street, observed Stride with someone in reality outside Dutfield's Yard. Her frame have become later discovered. The man have become described as being in his past due twenties with a darkish complexion, a small darkish moustache and a small dark hairstyle. He measured approximately five ft seven inches tall and wore darkish clothes and a deerstalker cap. He did no longer say a few issue because the couple did no longer do anything to elevate suspicions from PC Smith. Liz Stride great had a few minutes left.

A guy named Israel Schwartz changed into walking down Berner Street closer to the International Working Men's Educational Club. This is a social membership for Jewish employees. A guy about five'5" and 5" tall, with a trustworthy complexion and a small brown moustache, grow to be on foot a distance earlier. His face modified into whole and he appeared to be barely below the effect of alcohol. Schwartz positioned because the individual approached Schwartz, who come to be popularity at the entrance to Dutfield's outdoor. After a few terms, the man or woman tried to drag the lady onto the road. He then spun her round and driven the girl to the floor.

Schwartz believed he become witnessing domestic violence. He refused to get involved and crossed the road. He noticed a second man standing within the shadows lighting his pipe. Schwartz became passing him even as the character attacking the lady shouted "Lipski!" This second guy commenced following Schwartz, panicking and going for walks.

This story may be shared through way of Israel Schwartz to every the police and the media later. He turn out to be now not able to talk English so he wanted to talk via a translator. This may additionally moreover have added approximately a few data getting out of region in translation. His tale turn out to be retold numerous instances and it changed into nearly disregarded through the police.

What can we make of this tale a century later than it became? Schwartz seems to don't have any cause to make up this fictitious story. It is possible that the person Schwartz observed attacking Elizabeth Stride may additionally moreover genuinely be Jack the Ripper. What approximately the second guy? Do we consider the Ripper had an companion in this crime? Evidence shows in any other case. The proof suggests otherwise. Chief Inspector Swanson, however, stated in a document published October 19, 1888 that police had positioned the "second guy" and cleared him from any involvement inside the murder.

Schwartz observed the person attacking Elizabeth Stride by myself. It is feasible that Schwartz misread the situation in panic. Schwartz discovered the altercation and modified into 15 minutes later "Long Liz" could grow to be Jack the Ripper's 1/three sufferer.

Louis Diemshutz have become the steward for the International Working Men's Educational Club. He had previously been at Westow Hill Market, in which he ran a stall promoting less expensive rings, on the equal time as he lower back to Dutfield's Yard. His pony reacted and refused to transport further as he entered the outside. Diemshutz noticed the motive of the horse's distress through the usage of looking into the darkness. A crumpled shape lay at the floor near the membership wall. He attempted to poke it together along with his whip however no results so he have been given off the horse and went to investigate.

It have become windy that night, so Diemshutz lit a wholesome. However, the gust rapid extinguished it. He have become capable of see a girl's form after a brief flash of flame. He ran into the club looking for help. He stated, "There's an elderly girl mendacity in the backyard," to startled club members. But, he could not answer the query proper now. Diemshutz once more to the outdoor with numerous membership members. He used the candle as a beacon. However, it furnished enough mild to appearance the terrible injuries inflicted upon the female's throat. Diemshutz, collectively with the alternative club members, right away dispersed to search for a constable. Their cries of "Murder!" & "Police!" speedy attracted PC Edward Spooner's hobby. A crowd of fifteen people had already assembled by the time Spooner and the enterprise again to their backyard. Spooner reached proper down to look at the victim and discovered that her pores and skin modified into nonetheless warm.

Spooner lifted the sufferer's chin to appearance her throat, which he later called "fearfully" lessen.

Elizabeth Stride

Constables Henry Lamb (left) and Edward Collins (right) were the subsequent police officers to attain at Dutfield's Yard. Lamb ordered them to transport again to Dutfield's Yard after the institution had grown to 30. He warned that if blood changed into on their clothes they may be asked tough questions. He ordered Collins to go fetch Dr. Frederick William Blackwell, who lives close by at a hundred Commercial Street. Morris Eagle, one the club people emerge as then despatched to Leman Street Police Station for further help.

Dr. Blackwell arrived at the Yard at 1:06 a.M., and after quick exam declared the female useless. He additionally said that the lady had in all likelihood died among 20-half-hour earlier. The cause of dying have turn out to be a intense reduce to the neck. It commenced out on the left and went thru all of the blood vessels. It then cut right through the windpipe, completing on the opposite aspect. Dr. Blackwell stated that the killer grabbed the sufferer with the aid of her scarf round her neck, pulled her backwards after which slit her vocal chords and windpipe. She might probably have died internal 90 seconds due to the severity of her wound.

The police arrived at the scene and started out to manner the scene while Dr. Blackwell emerge as nonetheless analyzing the corpse. These measures were now not not unusual in the ones days. However, PC Lamb changed into able to command that Dutfield's Yard's gates be closed with all outsiders. He and PC Collins then made their way via the gang, looking for blood on clothing and palms. The pair then searched the membership, earlier than going to the cottages backing onto the club and waking the residents. Nobody had ever seen or heard whatever.

Lamb and Collins were lower decrease back by the time Inspectors West, Pinhorn, and Dr. Phillips arrived. After a short assembly between the two medical doctors, and senior officers of the police, the time it took to die changed into decreased to sixteen mins among 12:36 a.M. And 12:fifty six A.M. Louis Diemshutz appeared to have interrupted the Ripper's paintings and left his bloodlust unsatiated. This would have had horrible results for a few unique woman, unluckily.

Entrance to Dutfield's Yard

Kate Eddowes Comes to Grief

The Mitre Square Atrocity

Mitre Square is a small cobble-stoned rectangular measuring 24 yards with the resource of 24. It is surrounded by way of way of warehouses and business homes, with a few houses. The Square lies inside the City of London's bounds and is simplest 1 / 4 of a mile (or twenty minutes) from Dutfield's Yard. It turn out to be darkish and remoted at night time time even as all the groups had been closed. It will be the scene of an abominable homicide inside the early hours of September 30, 1888.

Mitre Square

Catherine Eddowes, much like the other 3 Ripper sufferers was additionally a prostitute.

She have become additionally an alcoholic, who spent most of her profits on alcohol and changed into identified for eccentric conduct. This changed into what were given her in trouble on September twenty ninth even as she became arrested at Aldgate High Street. She had entertained a crowd with a drunken imitation fireside engine. She become taken to Bishopsgate Police Station and located in a cellular.

The following couple of hours were spent fast asleep via Catherine, or Kate, as she was affectionately regarded. By 12:15 she become aware over again and creating a song a sultry music. PC George Hutt have become the officer on responsibility and went to her cellular to inform her to pipe down. Kate then demanded at the same time as she might be released. Hutt answered, "When you're able to attend to yourself," Eddowes spoke back, "I can do it now."

PC Hutt end up in truth not satisfied with the beneficial useful resource of this assertion as he stored Kate in his keep for 40 greater minutes earlier than ultimately releasing her at 12:fifty five AM. She then requested Hutt even as it modified into. Hutt stated, "Too beyond because of get any greater beverages.". Kate said, "I receives a damned appropriate hiding after I get lower back domestic," and Hutt agreed that she probable deserved it. He stated,

"You do not have the right to drink." Kate spoke back with "Good night oldcock" as she set out in the direction of Houndsditch. She followed a path that would take her to Mitre Square in 8 minutes. The killer of Elizabeth Stride, who turned into coming from the alternative route, come to be also on her way to the rectangular at that moment.

PC Edward Watkins became one of the officers who walked the Aldgate beat on that night time time. Watkins' path passed through Mitre Square as quickly as every twelve to fourteen minutes. When he came through the vicinity at 1:30 AM, he shined his lantern across the quadrant and noticed now not some thing uncommon.

After leaving the Imperial Club, Harry Harris, Joseph Hyam Levy, and Joseph Lawende walked along Duke Street for a few minutes. They noticed a couple on foot alongside Church Street. The female have become shielding the man's hand while the individual spoke to her. Harris and Levy had been now not able to perceive the character and paid little hobby to the couple.

Joseph Lawende became, however, greater attentive. Later, he might swear that the female he noticed wasn't Catherine Eddowes.

Lawende changed into in a position, notwithstanding horrible street lights, to offer an in depth description of the character. According to Lawende, the person turn out to be approximately 30 years vintage, medium-sized, and honest-skinned. He wore a free-turning into jacket and a grey fabric cap. He wore a crimson neckerchief round his neck. Given that Lawende pleasant had a very short view of the person, this description turn out to be extraordinarily thorough. Although he have end up in all likelihood flawed on a few elements, Catherine Eddowes' corpse become found clearly 15 mins later in Mitre Square. This indicates that Joseph Lawende can also had been one of the few who observed the face of Jack the Ripper.

Just mins after Joseph Lawende noticed the couple speaking collectively at 1:forty four AM, PC Edward Watkins become already returned on his circle path and entering into Mitre Square. He'd visible nothing uncommon while he had surpassed via the place fifteen mins in advance than. He made a horrible discovery as he pointed his flashlight proper right right into a darkish nook.

The female's body lay flat on the ground. Her toes were managing in the path of the rectangular. Her garments have been pulled above her waist. Her stomach became reduce, her throat grow to be lessen and her belly split open. Her intestines protruded from the wound. Her face come to be moreover significantly lacerated and blood have become pooling round it.

Watkins screamed in horror after which spun spherical to race at some stage in the rectangular toward Tonge and Kearley's warehouse. There he met George Morris, a retired officer from the police strain. Watkins shouted, "Please help me!" Here's some exclusive lady torn to quantities.

The night time watchman grabbed his lamp and followed Watkins in the course of the rectangular to the southwest corner. He took one look at Watkins' body before sprinting alongside Mitre Street in Aldgate route, blowing furiously along together with his whistle. The ruckus fast caught the eye of Holland and Harvey, who rather to Mitre Square with him to peer the bloody scene. Holland ran to Dr. George Sequeira's house on Jewry Street nearby.

Sequeira arrived on the scene at 1:fifty five. He failed to problem to test for a pulse and declared that loss of existence come to be straight away. He moreover said that he did not agree with the killer had any anatomical competencies. The City Police Divisional Surgeon Dr. Frederick Gordon Brown arrived to perform an intensive postmortem detailing the terrible nature of the crime. Brown's opinion on the extent of anatomical know-how of the killer emerge as substantially distinct from Sequeira. Brown believed that the killer had "large understanding about the region of organs within the belly hollow area and the way to dispose of them."

Catherine Eddowes

In the period in-between, Inspector Edward Collard arrived at Bishopsgate Police Station. He ordered a right away attempting to find and door-to-door inquiries had been made within the location of Mitre Square. Superintendent James McWilliam arrived subsequent with a hard and rapid of his men. He without delay dispersed them to appearance the Spitalfields streets, accommodations homes, and extraordinary regions. They met numerous guys alongside their path, and all had been stopped and interrogated to no avail. It regarded that the killer had in reality vanished.

Ironically, Richard Pearse, a City of London Police Constable, modified into the best man or woman living in Mitre Square at that component. Pearse hadn't seen or heard a few detail. George Morris, night time watchman who had sounded alarm, had moreover not visible or heard a few aspect.

It modified into referred to within the Illustrated Police News:

"He (Morris), may want to concentrate the footsteps and velocity of the policeman, so it seemed not viable that the lady should have made any sounds without him noticing them. He most effective remarked to a policeman on that night time time time that he wanted that the "butcher" may additionally want to go to Mitre Square and deliver him a assisting hand; but the butcher had already arrived and he become certainly blind to it.

Even stranger become the clean fact that Catherine, at the appropriate 2d Catherine arrived, turn out to be already asleep.

Eddowes entered Mitre Square together with her assassin. Three City detectives, Robert Outram and Daniel Halse, were taking walks round Mitre Street near the rectangular, but noticed no longer something.

For post-mortem, the body of Catherine Eddowes had to be eliminated and brought to Golden Lane

The exam come to be completed by using the use of Dr. Brown at Mortuary. Like Polly Nichols or Annie Chapman's throats, Eddowes had been deeply slit from left to proper. Although the wound delivered on lack of life, Dr. Brown's testimony brilliant describes excessive postmortem mutilations.

"The stomach changed into uncovered from the breast bone to wherein the pubes have been. Two ft of colon have become eliminated and the intestines had been severed. The peritoneal membrane grow to be removed and the left kidney grow to be carefully eliminated. The left renal vein have come to be additionally reduce. It modified into done through a person who need to have regarded the location of the kidney. The stump modified into 3/four inch in diameter. Some of the ligaments were removed from the rest of the womb. The vaginal and cervical wombs were unharmed.

"The face modified into appreciably mutilated. The lower left eyelid emerge as divided via a 1/4 inch lessen. The right eyelid became sliced to about half of inch. The bridge of the nose changed into reduce to a depth of approximately 1/2 of inch. It ran from the left edge of the nasal bone, near the thoughts-set of proper-element jaw. The nose tip emerge as very detached from the nostril.

"Several outstanding cuts have been made to her face. The right earlobe modified into moreover severed. She had fallen from her garments even as she have become taken into the morgue."

Dr. Brown concluded that the killer knew exactly which organs he desired, and had extricated them with precision.

Chapter 12: The Writing At The Wall

A Strip of Apron, and the Goulston Street Graffito

The Whitechapel Murderer, who had murdered Catherine Eddowess, fled east from Mitre Square along Aldgate. Although this seems ordinary considering the style of police officers inside the area, the Ripper turn out to be in truth confident that he must outmaneuver his pursuers in a place he knew properly. How are we capable to show that he traveled east? A piece of evidence grow to be found in Goulston Street's doorway, it sincerely is only some blocks from Mitre Square.

PC Alfred Long observed the clue in a bloody apron strip at the identical time as taking walks along Goulston Street at 2.Fifty five AM at the morning of the homicide. Later, it turn out to be decided that the cloth were taken from Catherine Eddowes's apron whilst she died. It might be that the killer took it to smooth his arms and his blade. PC

Long had certainly walked past the identical spot at 2.20 and no longer observed some thing unusual. Detective Daniel Halse had additionally exceeded the identical spot at 2:20 and had not found some element uncommon. This shows that the killer dropped it amongst 2:20 to 2:fifty five, approximately half of of of an hour to as a minimum one hour after Catherine Eddowes' demise. This tells us plenty approximately Ripper. He emerge as confident that he ought to preserve one step in advance and now not allow down the police. He ought to not have stayed on the streets with the City of London police institution looking him. Psychopaths are stated for their danger-looking for behaviour.

Another problem of the crimes is determined with the aid of the usage of the apron strip. It have become at the start believed that the Ripper is probably covered in blood after he had completed his gory mutilations. A clean assessment of the evidence indicates in any other case. We can see that the small piece of material he took from his apron suggests that he didn't have any blood to clean up. How have to that be? It's actually quite easy.

Nowadays, it is significantly normal that the Ripper smothered his sufferers to loss of life. The victim changed into both dead by the time he commenced reducing or their hearts had slowed so much that there has been no blood spurt or inclined blood spurt. All crime scenes had this statement. It is possible that he have come to be wearing an overcoat while mutilating the victims. He eliminated it in advance than he achieved the homicide. This changed into ostensibly to permit him to have intercourse alongside with his sufferer. He might then located the overcoat returned on and cover any bloodstains. He walked out of the Annie Chapman crime scene at daytime, following a route that exceeded the Spitalfields

Market and yet he end up now not suspicious.

This strip of apron answers many questions on the Ripper's approach of operation and might additionally show display some information approximately his persona. There emerge as another clue that night that became discovered, and it answers as many questions due to the fact the apron.

This is the famous graffito that changed into scrawled on the Goulston Street wall. It became proper above the vicinity in which the piece of apron have become placed. It changed into written in chalk and take a look at:

"The Juwes will not be held accountable for whatever."

This one line of semi-literate scrawl has attracted some of hobby. Is it feasible that it modified into written with the useful useful resource of the Ripper? If so, for what motive? Three viable reasons have been supplied.

The message changed into now not despatched with the useful resource of manner of the murderer. He tossed the apron apart and it ended up beside the meaningless graffiti. This message had no longer whatever to do the case.

The 2nd modified into that the message were written thru the killer, and became a shape of triumphalism. He come to be so happy with his double homicide success, he boasted to the police at the same time as concurrently identifying himself as Jew. Even although it have become endorsed that Juwes become the Yiddish spelling for Jews on the time, this have grow to be rapid disproved via the leader Rabbi.

Scotland Yard desired the very last interpretation that the killer presupposed to divert interest from himself. Although he wasn't a Jew, he knew that many locals believed the murders were the art work of "foreigners." Therefore, he wrote the message to inflame anti-Semitism. This precept have become supported with the resource of the reality that maximum of the homes on which he wrote the message have been domestic to single Jewish guys. This concept modified into popular via the investigators and fueled the controversial next step inside the studies.

The be counted have become introduced to the eye of Sir Charles Warren, Police Commissioner. Warren arrived on the internet website to look at it at 5:30 a.M. He right away supported the Metropolitan Police. The message have grow to be to be deleted right now, and no photograph taken to preserve it.

This was a crucial clue that might have found out Jack the Ripper's identification.

Warren later justified his moves in a document to Home place of business on

November 6, 1888. He come to be concerned about the possibility of Gentiles seeing the message and launching violent retribution. He felt there has been no manner to lose the message, as it might rapid emerge as visible and streets would possibly fill up with human beings.

Is Warren correct to do that? In retrospect, it appears he became. Many those who located the message stated that it become pretty diminished, and consequently no longer of recent age. It is likewise now not probable that Ripper may want to have been visible in open writing a message on the wall, whilst police searched the area for him. The controversy surrounding the message being erased could speedy be overshadowed via some other Ripper letter, this one marked "From Hell."

Dear Boss

Letters from Hell

Two letters had been specially first rate inside the Jack the Ripper research. However, the police and newspapers received over seven hundred at some point of the research. While numerous the ones letters were despatched via worried citizens, offering recommendations and recommendation on the way to capture Jack the Ripper, a massive extensive variety (three hundred) modified into purportedly from Jack himself.

Most of those letters have been hoaxes and are rightfully criticized. However, this does not imply that they have been all insignificant. The "Dear Boss", a letter addressed to the Central News Agency that arrived on September 27, gave the killer his famous nickname. The unidentified killer grow to be referred to as "Whitechapel Murderer", "Red Fiend," or "Leather Apron" preceding to the murders in Elizabeth Stride and Catherine Eddowes, September 30, 1888. But the Dear Boss correspondence supplied a extra catchy notion. The letter became signed "Jack the Ripper" and the killer may be remembered for his terrifying nom de guerre.

Dear Boss Letter

Initial remedy for the "Dear Bosss" letter became similar to that given to the crank letters regarding the case. The police were forced to examine the letter more cautiously after the double homicide.

The letter said that the killer desired to go to paintings right away if he had the threat. It regarded that he had completed exactly that. He threatened to clip the following technique he did. "Take the woman's ears and supply them to the Police officers, most effective for jolly wouldn't you?" One of Catherine Eddowes' earlobes have become indeed removed. That regarded too near twist of fate. The killer had clearly written the letter?

The difficulty grow to be now not well-received thru senior law enforcement officials. The studies modified into proving difficult and that they have been task to harsh criticism from the media. With the general public outraged on the modern-day murders, and with out a clue to discover, they decided to provide the letter to the papers. Maybe someone will recognize the handwriting and pick out up the uncommon diction.

It turn out to be honestly so the complete "Dear Bosss" letter regarded in all number one London dailies on October 1. This delivered about a flood of recent guidelines, further to masses of hoax letters. One of these changed right into a postcard that arrived at Central News Agency on Monday October 1.

The card became written in purple ink, and end up signed in a fashion just like the "Dear Boss" letter. It become moreover included with bloodstains. It have become stamped with a October 1 postmark and take a look at as follows:

"I wasn't codding luxurious antique Boss, after I gave the quit, you could listen about Saucyjacky's artwork the next day double-event this time number one squealed slightly could not end right now had now not the time for police to get ears. Thank you on your very last letter. I obtained it at artwork.

Jack the Ripper"

These terms propose that the killer wrote them unexpectedly after killing Liz Stride, Kate Eddowes, and earlier than the murders have become public. This appeared to confirm its authenticity, so it come to be decided to put up it once more. This tactic proved to be disastrous as police acquired a flood of fake tips and hoaxes. These hoaxes needed to be looked after out. This took away treasured manpower from distinct avenues of research.

The case changed into now not shifting ahead in October, and as such extra letters started out to reach in mailboxes of newsmen and law enforcement officials. On October sixteen, a letter arrived at Mr. George Lusk's residence, the President of Mile End Vigilance Committee. It is the maximum well-known Ripper letter, and it changed into addressed "From Hell".

Lusk is, of route, a distinguished determine internal Ripper folklore. After the "double occasion", his committee commenced on foot patrols inside the vicinity. Lusk had spoken at several public gatherings, and changed into regardless of the fact that soliciting the Home Secretary to reconsider the "no rewards" insurance. Lusk emerge as additionally featured in severa newspapers speakme about the case.

All this exposure attracted unwanted interest. Lusk stated to police in October that he come to be being located by way of using a "mysterious stranger". He additionally acquired two letters claiming to be from Jack the Ripper. On Tuesday, October sixteen, Lusk was furnished with a small bundle deal wrapped in brown paper, bearing a London stamp. It rapid have turn out to be apparent why the package deal deal had an uncommon heady scent. The package deal contained 1/2 of of a human kidney. A letter have emerge as also located inner, which said:

"From hell

Mr Lusk

Sor

I will ship you half of the Kidne that I got from one female. If you're able to entice me as quickly as I can, I will ship you the whole thing.

Mishter Lusk"

From Hell letter

Lusk to start with concept the letter have end up a sick shaggy canine tale and that the kidney had in all likelihood come from an animal. He decided to get a clinical opinion. Thus, he took the package deal deal to Mile End Road, in which Dr. Reed examined it and determined that the kidney end up human. However, he recommended that Lusk are seeking out for a second opinion. The kidney changed into then taken to London Hospital, wherein Dr. Thomas Openshaw (the Pathological Curator) tested it.

Openshaw confirmed that the specimen is surely human, however stated that it modified into no longer possible to prove who it got here from or whether it have become a person. Openshaw believed that the specimen changed into more likely to have come from a cadaver obtained for medical dissection. He additionally endorsed that the prank grow to be perpetrated in component by means of the use of a scientific student.

However, to the media, the confirmation that a kidney changed into human modified into all that modified into vital. The "From Hell" letter contained a proposal of cannibalism and a macabre twist. The papers posted erroneous variations of Dr. Openshaw's evaluation over the subsequent days. According to the papers, the kidney belonged to a lady elderly forty five and "no longer but 3 week useless", who became a heavy drinker who desired gin. Undoubtedly, this end up intended to indicate that the kidney belonged to Kate Eddowes. However, Dr. Openshaw by no means supplied that opinion.

Dr. Gordon Brown become the following to look at the kidney. He is a pathologist linked at the City Police Force. Although he additionally believed the kidney become human, he did now not offer any records about its origins. This may were now not feasible in that time period. However, he did trust Openshaw's assessment of the whole affair as a hoax perpetrated essentially via a medical pupil.

A very last misconception concerning the kidney must be dispelled. In pretty quite a range of books, it's far been said that the kidney showed signs and symptoms of superior Bright's sickness. This is the equal situation that Kate Eddowes became supposed to have suffered from. This reality has been substantially referred to and is now trendy as fact. The origins of the tale aren't easy. It is concept that it originated in the memoirs Major Henry Smith, an acting City Commissioner. Smith credit rating this evaluation to Mr. Sutton who is a London Hospital senior health care issuer and an professional on kidney ailments.

Sutton's written reports have now not survived to useful resource Smith's claims, if they have been ever made in any respect. It appears that Major Smith modified into no longer prone to exaggeration and had a reputation of being a chunk reasonably priced with the truth even as it got here within the way an brilliant story. The majority of doctors who tested the kidney at the time believed it to be from Catherine Eddowes. They aren't validly 2nd-guessed.

What about the Ripper letters? Did any of them come from Jack? It isn't viable to show that they've been. Thomas J. Bulling has been recognized as the author of the "Dear Boss" letter. Bulling modified right into a journalist who labored for Central News Agency. Who is aware of what passed off to the "Letter from Hell"? Hoax letter writing have emerge as nearly a country huge obsession in some unspecified time within the destiny of Ripper's research. There is not any cause to believe this letter became more real than masses of others.

Chapter 13: Mary Kelly's Horrific Murder

Whitechapel changed into yet again in a country of digital lockdown for the following weeks. Many prostitutes fled the location to discover hotels with their pals and family, leaving inside the back of the as quickly as bustling streets. Also, valid change changed into affected. Many Londoners were scared to even set foot in Whitechapel for worry of being enslaved through a monster whose legend had reached near mythic proportions.

The police spoke back with a fervent response. Officers in plainclothes and uniforms flooded the place, on foot alongside the streets at night time time. They were assisted with the aid of the use of Mr. Lusk's Mile End Vigilance Committee who employed close by guys with police whistles and billy golf equipment to patrol darkened alleyways and yards.

Police officials worked day and night time time to find out the splendid inns places within the area. More than 2,000 lodgers were interrogated, with specific interest given to folks who worked in positive occupations. A desired of 76 butchers, slaughterers, and sailors who paintings on the Thames River boats had been all interrogated. In the want of finding the killer, a collection of bloodhounds were additionally deployed.

The government moreover disbursed 80,000 handbills within the location: "POLICE NOTICE

TO THE OCCUPIER Friday 31 August, Saturday eighth and Sunday 30 September 1888 were the times while girls were attacked in Whitechapel with the useful resource of a suspect from the instantaneous place. If you've got were given any suspicions about virtually anybody, please inform the closest Metropolitan Police Office (30 September 1888) if you understand.

This brought about a flood of latest leads, masses of which got here from indignant higher halves or jilted fanatics who had cautioned their companions in spite. It did no longer yield any real clues.

None of these techniques helped within the seize of Jack. However, they did have the effect of calming Whitechapel tensions. One month went through without every other homicide. Slowly, the streets lower once more to everyday and prostitutes resumed their profession. Whitechapel's humans believed the Ripper had left, however they were about be confirmed incorrect within the maximum brutal style.

Mary Kelly, a 25-three hundred and sixty five days vintage Irish prostitute who arrived in London from Limerick, have become described as Mary Kelly. Mary modified into defined as tall and excellent through manner of using individuals who knew her. The Daily Telegraph later added that she have become "truthful in complexion, with light hair and had quite attractive abilities." Mary is likewise nicely-desired and respected in the region. Many spoke as an alternative of her powerful demeanor. However, some stated that she may be abusive beneath the have an impact on.

Mary rented a room at the primary ground at Miller's Court, Dorset Street, Spitalfields. However, at the begin November 1888 she end up plagued by way of cash issues and changed into several weeks behind on her lease. Joe Barnett, her lover, have end up also unemployed and broke. Kelly and Barnett had a recent argument, and he had moved out of their shared mattress room. The spat ended speedy. Barnett visited Mary at Miller's Court on Thursday, November eight and apologized for his behavior and that he didn't have any cash for her. He grow to be able to spend about an hour with Mary earlier than leaving spherical 7:45 to move back to Bishopsgate. He performed some rounds of whisky with the opposite residents, earlier than retiring spherical 12:30.

Mary Kelly's bed room in Miller's Court

Mary Kelly became contacted via John, her landlord, at 10:forty five AM the following morning.

McCarthy sent Thomas Bowyer, his assistant to Mary's Court, to gather Mary's lease. Bowyer arrived at Miller's Court, wherein he banged on the door times but obtained no reaction. He believed Mary emerge as hiding in the mattress room and he went to the window to see the broken pane. He reached for the curtain's component and pulled it apart, accomplishing thru. He staggered again, looking ashen-confronted, moments later. He grew to come to be spherical and ran. Bowyer stumbled via the door because of the truth Landlord John McCarthy, his neighbor, became there. He mumbled, "Guv'nor." Bowyer mumbled, "I think you will satisfactory come take a look." Bowyer became requested for additonal statistics and stated that there was "hundreds of blood." They then ran collectively in the direction of Miller's Court.

McCarthy believed that his assistant turn out to be incorrect or exaggerating. McCarthy rapid misplaced religion in his assistant's potential to look the interior of the darkened room. Mary Kelly's bed room changed into harking back to an abattoir. The bloody wall within the back of Mary Kelly's bed modified into apparent, and the gory pile of human flesh that changed into at the bedside table regarded locate it irresistible became crafted from human flesh. This wasn't the worst factor. The mattress emerge as curious approximately the beneficial useful resource of a frame that lay so bloody and so badly mutilated it may slightly be identified as a human.

McCarthy fought lower lower again, taking in extra air and seeking to avoid ejecting his breakfast onto a hard floor. McCarthy later stated to a journalist that he could not get rid of the sight. "It regarded more like a devilish work than someone."

John McCarthy took some time to regain his composure. He in the end regained his composure and despatched Bowyer to the nearby Commercial Street Police Station that allows you to get a police officer. Bowyer stumbled thru the door as Beck and Inspector Dew were talking inside the station. Bowyer managed to break out through pronouncing, "It's The Ripper." "He's done some different."

Soon, Beck and Dew followed Bowyer lower decrease back to Dorset Street.

They attempted to lock the door when they arrived at Miller's Court. Inspector Beck went to the window and regarded into the room. He speedy retreated. He endorsed his colleague, "For God's sake Dew,".

Dew did but appearance and took in a view that would live with him for the relaxation his lifestyles. He defined it fifty years later in his memoirs:

"As I expect again to Miller's Court and the occasions there, my antique nausea, indignation, and horror overwhelms me. It stays as vividly visible in my thoughts as it modified into the previous day. There could not had been a extra brutal savage. It is not viable for any wild animal to do some thing as horrendous."

Dew summoned Inspector Abberline to the scene. He arrived within the enterprise Dr. George Bagster Phillips, a police preferred practitioner. The officers acquired a key from John McCarthy and entered the small, cluttered area wherein Mary's corpse lay. Even a veteran officer like Abberline and a skilled healthcare expert like Phillips placed it tough to see the corpse. Mary have become so badly disfigured that Joe Barnett, her lover, changed into now not capable of pick out out the body.

www.ingramcontent.com/pod-product-compliance
Lightning Source LLC
Chambersburg PA
CBHW070556010526
44118CB00012B/1335